PROTECTION OF ASSETS

INFORMATION SECURITY

PROTECTION
OF ASSETS

INFORMATION SECURITY

INTERNATIONAL
Advancing Security Worldwide®

ASIS International | 1625 Prince Street | Alexandria, VA 22314 USA | *www.asisonline.org*

FSC
www.fsc.org

MIX
Paper from
responsible sources
FSC® C015782

ACKNOWLEDGMENTS

ASIS International (ASIS), the world's leading society for security professionals, originally founded in 1955 as the American Society for Industrial Security, acquired *Protection of Assets* in December 2003. The acquisition of this work underscores the Society's leadership role in professional education. It is the sincere desire of ASIS and its editorial staff to continue to enhance the value of this important reference.

Protection of Assets, which has been in existence since 1974, is recognized as the premier reference for security professionals and the publisher wishes to acknowledge the two founding authors and subsequent editors.

Timothy J. Walsh, CPP   **Richard J. Healy, CPP**

———

Timothy L. Williams, CPP
Managing Editor

Editorial Associates

David G. Aggleton, CPP
Milton E. Moritz, CPP
Mike Hodge, J.D.
Sanford Sherizon, Ph.D., CISSP
Timothy J. Walsh, CPP, Editor Emeritus

As we move forward, confronted with issues that present a challenge to the security industry, our mission is to ensure that *Protection of Assets* provides the strategic solutions necessary to help professionals meet the demands of the 21st century and beyond. We also pledge to assemble a group of subject matter experts who will enhance this manual as necessary to achieve our mission.

Michael E. Knoke, CPP
Managing Editor

Eva Giercuszkiewicz, MLS, Project Manager
Evangeline Pappas, Production Manager
Peter E. Ohlhausen, Technical Editor

OBJECTIVES OF *PROTECTION OF ASSETS*

This *Protection of Assets (POA)* reference work is provided for a single, basic reason: the previous unavailability of such a comprehensive resource.

Although the availability of security literature is growing rapidly, with general and specialized texts, it has not been possible—until now—for a business manager or protection professional to find current, accurate, and practical treatment of the broad range of protection subjects, strategies, and solutions in a single source.

The need for such a comprehensive resource is quite widespread according to the editors, writers, and many professional colleagues whose advice has been sought in compiling this text. The growing size and frequency of all forms of asset losses, coupled by the related increasing cost and the complexity of countermeasures selection, demand a systematic and unified presentation of protection doctrine in all relevant areas, as well as standards and specifications as they are issued. Of course, it would be presumptuous to assume that any small group of authors could present such material unaided. It is, therefore, a fundamental objective of *Protection of Assets* to draw upon as large a qualified source base as can be developed. The writers, peer reviewers, and editors attempt to distill from the available data, common or recurrent characteristics, trends and other factors, which identify or signal valid protection strategies. The objective is to provide a source document where information on any protection problem can be obtained.

READERSHIP

Protection of Assets is intended for a wide readership: all security professionals and business managers with asset protection responsibility. The coherent discussion and pertinent reference material in each subject area should help the reader conduct unique research that is effective and organized. Of particular significance are the various forms, matrices, and checklists that give the reader a practical start toward application of the security theory to his or her own situation. *POA* also serves as a central reference for students pursuing a program in security or asset protection.

DIALOGUE

We hope that *Protection of Assets* becomes an important source of professional insight for those who read it and that it stimulates serious dialogue between and among security professionals. Any reader who is grappling with an unusual, novel, or difficult security problem and would appreciate the opinions of others is encouraged to write a succinct statement describing the problem and send it to us at ASIS [protectionofassets@asisonline.org]. At the reader's request his identity will not be disclosed, but the problem will be published with invitations for comment. Readers are also encouraged to communicate agreement or disagreement with strategies or applications recommended in *POA* and to suggest alternatives. We reserve the right to publish or refrain from publishing submitted material. The editors also solicit statements of reader opinion on matters of asset protection policy in which a cross-sectional view would be helpful.

SUPPLEMENTAL TRAINING

Readers with supervisory or management responsibility for other security and asset protection personnel will find *POA* to be a useful resource from which to assign required readings. Such readings could be elements of a formal training syllabus and could be assigned as part of related course sessions.

With all these objectives in mind, we present to you *Protection of Assets*, in the sincere belief it will enhance your expertise in the security field.

Michael E. Knoke, CPP
Managing Editor

CONTRIBUTORS

The success of this publication is directly related to the peer review process recognized by most professions. Security professionals, members of academia, and other subject matter experts were involved in contributing current information, conducting research, reviewing submissions, and providing constructive comments so that we are able to provide a publication that is recognized as the "go to" reference for security professionals worldwide.

It is with sincere appreciation that I wish to thank the below-named individuals who contributed to *Protection of Assets*.

Teresa M. Abrahamsohn, CPP

Sean A. Ahrens, CPP

Marene N. Allison

Randy I. Atlas, CPP

George J. Barletta, CPP

Mark H. Beaudry, CPP

Regis W. Becker, CPP

Brent Belcoff, CPP

Howard J. Belfor, CPP

Adolfo M. Benages, CPP

Lawrence K. Berenson, CPP

Alexander E. Berlonghi

Raymond J. Bernard, PSP

Henri A. Berube

Martin T. Biegelman, J.D.

Daniel E. Bierman, CPP, PSP

Patrick C. Bishop, CPP

Dennis R. Blass, CPP, PSP

Keith C. Blowe, CPP

Paul F. Boyarin, CPP, PCI

Tom Boyer

Pete Brake, Jr., CPP

Darryl R. Branham, CPP

Joseph P. Buckley, III

Jason Caissie, CPP, PSP

Lucien G. Canton, CPP

James P. Carino, Jr., CPP

Sue Carioti

James S. Cawood, CPP, PCI, PSP

Steve Chambers, CPP, PSP

Richard E. Chase, CPP

John C. Cholewa, III, CPP

Tom M. Conley, CPP

Geoffrey T. Craighead, CPP

Michael A. Crane, J.D., CPP

Bruce A. Dean, CPP

Fritz X. Delinski

Edward P. De Lise, CPP

David A. Dobbins, PSP

Colin Doniger, CPP, PSP

Clifford E. Dow, CPP

Christina M. Duffey, CPP

Brandon Dunlap

Nick Economou

Cheryl D. Elliott, CPP, PCI

James W. Ellis, CPP, PSP

William R. Etheridge

Gregory Alan Ewing, CPP, PSP

Kenneth G. Fauth, CPP

Lawrence J. Fennelly

Donald J. Fergus

Eugene F. Ferraro, CPP, PCI

James H. Fetzer, III, CPP

Michael T. Flachs, CPP

Linda F. Florence, Ph.D., CPP

Richard H. Frank, CPP

Kenneth M. Freeman, CPP

Peter J. French, CPP

Mary Lynn Garcia, CPP

John W. Gehrlein, CPP

Eva Giercuszkiewicz, MLS

Gregory A. Gilbert, CPP

Frederick G. Giles, CPP

Timothy D. Giles, CPP, PSP

David H. Gilmore, CPP

Christopher Giusti, CPP

Leo Gonnering, PSP

Brian D. Gouin, PSP

Richard P. Grassie, CPP

Benjamin P. Greer

Steven R. Harris

Ronald D. Heil, CPP

Ed Heisler, CPP, PSP

Richard J. Heffernan, CPP

Chris A. Hertig, CPP

William T. Hill, CPP

Ronald W. Hobbs, CPP

Mark D. Hucker, CPP

W. Geoffrey Hughes, PCI

John L. Hunepohl

Gregory L. Hurd, CPP

Gregory W. Jarpey, PSP

Sheila D. Johnson, CPP, PSP

Thomas R. Jost

Diane Horn Kaloustian

Cathy M. Kimble, CPP

R. Michael Kirchner, CPP

Glen W. Kitteringham, CPP

Michael E. Knoke, CPP

Terrence J. Korpal

James M. Kuehn, CPP

David Lam, CPP

Rich LaVelle, PSP

Robert F. Leahy, CPP, PSP

Robert E. Lee

Jeff Leonard, CPP, PSP

Todd P. Letcher

Emblez Longoria, CPP, PSP

Cynthia Long

Richard E. Maier, CPP

Loye A. Manning, CPP, PSP

Robert L. Martin, CPP

Ron Martin, CPP

Roger B. Maslen, CPP

Judith G. Matheny, CPP

Edward F. McDonough, Jr., CPP

Richard A. Michau, CPP

Bonnie S. Michelman, CPP

Owen J. Monaghan, CPP

Wayne Morris, CPP, PSP

Patrick M. Murphy, CPP, PSP

Carla Naude, CPP

James W. Nelson

Robert L. Oatman, CPP

Gerald A. O'Farrell, CPP

Peter E. Ohlhausen

Leonard Ong, CPP

Harm J. Oosten, CPP

S. Steven Oplinger

Denis A. O'Sullivan, CPP

Jaime P. Owens, CPP

Gerard P. Panaro, J.D.

James F. Pastor, Ph.D.

David G. Patterson, CPP, PSP

John T. Perkins, CPP

Karl S. Perman

Kevin E. Peterson, CPP

Charlie R. A. Pierce

Doug Powell, CPP, PSP

Patrick K. Quinn, CPP

Roy A. Rahn, CPP

John D. Rankin, CPP

William G. Rauen, CPP

David L. Ray, LL.B.

Joseph Rector, CPP, PCI, PSP

Ty L. Richmond, CPP

Lisa M. Ruth

Jeffrey J. Ryder, Jr., CPP, PSP

Mark A. Sanna, CPP

Stephen Saravara, III, J.D., CPP

Charles A. Sennewald, CPP

Dennis Shepp, CPP, PCI

Shari Shovlin

Marc Siegel, Ph.D.

Laurie Simmons, CPP, PSP

Dennis Smith, CPP

Stan Stahl, Ph.D.

Paul J. Steiner, Jr., CPP

Pamela M. Stewart, PCI

Dan E. Taylor, Sr., CPP

Lynn A. Thackery, CPP, PSP

Mark L. Theisen, CPP

Dave N. Tyson, CPP

Joann Ugolini, CPP, PSP

Darleen Urbanek

Mike VanDrongelen, CPP, PCI, PSP

Karim Vellani, CPP

Barry J. Walker, CPP

Michael W. Wanik, CPP

Roger D. Warwick, CPP

Fritz Weidner

Richard C. Werth, CPP

Allan R. Wick, CPP, PSP

Anthony S. Wilcox, CPP

Donald S. Williams, CPP

Reginald J. Williams, CPP

Richard F. Williams, CPP

Timothy L. Williams, CPP

Gavin Wilson, PSP

Coleman L. Wolf, CPP

Loftin Woodiel, CPP

Richard P. Wright, CPP

Allison Wylde

Richard Y. Yamamoto, CPP

Scott S. Young, CPP

TABLE OF CONTENTS

PREFACE

CONTRIBUTORS

Chapter 1. **INFORMATION ASSET PROTECTION** 1

1.1　Introduction 1
1.2　History of Espionage and Business Intelligence Collection 2
1.3　Risk Management Approach to IAP 4
　　1.3.1　Today's Global Information Environment 4
　　1.3.2　Threat Categories and Examples 5
　　1.3.3　Risk Assessment and Due Diligence 9
　　1.3.4　Attaining Buy-In 9
1.4　Approaches to Risk Mitigation 11
　　1.4.1　Basic Protection Practices 11
　　1.4.2　Physical Security 12
　　1.4.3　Personnel Security 15
　　1.4.4　Privacy Protection 15
　　1.4.5　Business Practices 16
　　1.4.6　Operations Security or Information Risk Management 17
　　1.4.7　Travel and Meeting Security 18
　　1.4.8　Preventing and Detecting Counterfeiting and Illegal Copying 20
1.5　Legal Protections 21
　　1.5.1　Copyrights 22
　　1.5.2　Trademarks, Trade Dress, and Service Marks 23
　　1.5.3　Patents 23
　　1.5.4　Trade Secrets 24
　　1.5.5　International Concerns 24
　　1.5.6　Nondisclosure Agreements and Contracts 25
1.6　Technical Protective Measures 26
　　1.6.1　Technical Surveillance Countermeasures 26
　　1.6.2　Protection in an IT Environment 26
　　1.6.3　Protection in Special Environments 28
1.7　Response and Recovery After an Information Loss 29
1.8　Summary 30
Appendix A:　Sample Policy on Information Asset Protection 31
Appendix B:　Quick Reference Guide for Information Asset Protection 39
Appendix C:　Sample Nondisclosure Agreements 43
Appendix D:　Technical Reports and Laboratory Notebooks 49
Appendix E:　Information Disposal and Destruction 55
References 57

Chapter 2. **THE INCREASING IMPORTANCE OF INFORMATION SYSTEMS SECURITY** 61

2.1   The Human Challenge: Failure of Imagination 62
2.2   State of Information Systems Security 64
2.3   Economics of Information Systems Security 68
2.4   Critical Success Factors 69
2.5   Implications to Physical Security in a Converged World 71
2.6   The Cybercrime Challenge: A National Challenge 78
References 81

Chapter 3. **THE INFORMATION SYSTEMS SECURITY BODY OF KNOWLEDGE** 85

3.1   The Elements of ISS Risk 86
     3.1.1   ISS Terms 86
     3.1.2   Fundamental Equation of ISS 87
     3.1.3   Information System Threats 87
     3.1.4   Information System Vulnerabilities 89
     3.1.5   Information System Control Objectives 90
     3.1.6   Information System Countermeasures 90
3.2   Down the Rabbit Hole: Computer Logic, System Complexity,
    and Inherent Vulnerability 93
     3.2.1   How Computer Systems Work 94
     3.2.2   Managing the IT Infrastructure 106
     3.2.3   Real World, Networked Computer Systems 107
     3.2.4   Additional Information Security Concepts 115
     3.2.5   Information Security Technologies 116
3.3   ISS Practitioner Frameworks 118
     3.3.1   ISO/IEC 27001:2005 and ISO/IEC 27002:2005 118
     3.3.2   CISSP Common Body of Knowledge 120
     3.3.3   Information Security Governance: Guidance
           for Boards of Directors and Executive Management 121
     3.3.4   Generally Accepted Information System
           Security Practices (GAISSP) 122
3.4   The Emerging Legal, Regulatory and Contractual
    Landscape Regarding ISS 123
     3.4.1   Payment Card Industry Data Security Standard (PCI DSS) 123
     3.4.2   Health Care and Insurance Portability and
           Accountability Act (HIPAA) 125
     3.4.3   Gramm-Leach-Bliley Act (GLBA) 126
     3.4.4   Children's Online Privacy Protection Act (COPPA) 127
     3.4.5   Sarbanes-Oxley Act (SOX) 128
     3.4.6   Red Flag Rules 129
     3.4.7   FTC Enforcement Actions 130

3.4.8   State Breach Disclosure and Related ISS and Privacy Laws   134

3.4.9   European Union Data Protection Directive   135

3.4.10   Emerging Case Law   136

3.5   Special Topics in ISS   139

3.5.1   ISS Risk and Vulnerability Assessment.   139

3.5.2   ISS Policy Implementation   141

3.5.3   Incident Response   142

3.6   Total ISS Management   144

3.6.1   ISO 27001 Information Security Management Systems   144

3.6.2   Making Continual Improvement Happen.   146

Appendix A: Information Systems Security Resources   149

References 155

Chapter 4. **SECURITY CHALLENGES OF CONVERGENCE**   159

4.1   Network Risk   159

4.1.1   Network Case Study 1: Camera System   160

4.1.2   Network Case Study 2: Access Control.   162

4.2   Communications Attacks   168

4.2.1   Social Engineering   169

4.2.2   Direct Hacking   169

4.2.3   Malware   170

4.2.4   Web Attacks   171

4.3   Information Security Management System   174

4.3.1   Security Policy   175

4.3.2   Organizing Information Systems Security.   176

4.3.3   Asset Management.   176

4.3.4   Human Resources Management   176

4.3.5   Physical and Environmental Security   176

4.3.6   Communications and Operations Management   177

4.3.7   Access Control   181

4.3.8   Information Systems Acquisition, Development,
          and Maintenance.   182

4.3.9   Information Security Incident Management   182

4.3.10   Business Continuity Management   182

4.3.11   Compliance   183

4.3.12   ISMS Summary.   183

4.4   Conclusion.   184

References   185

INDEX   187

TABLE OF FIGURES

2-1	Video-to-Recorder Layout.	72
2-2	Video Infrastructure	72
2-3	Basic Access Control Card Flow	74
2-4	Basic Wiegand Flow	75
2-5	Networked Access Control System.	76

3-1	ISS Overall Objectives and Control Objectives	90
3-2	Basic Components of Computer Operation.	95
3-3	Direct Communication	98
3-4	Communications by Router.	99
3-5	Computer Logic Entry Points	100
3-6	Authentication	103
3-7	AAA Triad	103
3-8	CIA Triad, Expanded.	104
3-9	Firewall	107
3-10	Virtual Private Network	108
3-11	Traditional PBX System	111
3-12	Phone Company Central Office	112
3-13	Voice-over-IP (VOIP) System	113
3-14	Information Security Management Maturity Level	122
3-15	Plan-Do-Check-Act Model Applied to ISMS Processes	145

4-1	Networked Video System	160
4-2	Networked Access Control System.	162
4-3	Access Control System Communication: Reader to Controller to Network	163
4-4	Access Control System Communication: Server to Network	163
4-5	Logical Communication Flow	164
4-6	Access Control Elements Connected to Switch.	165
4-7	Layer 2 Communication.	165
4-8	Access Control Router Communication.	166
4-9	Workstation to Access Control Server Data Flow.	167

CHAPTER 1
INFORMATION ASSET PROTECTION

1.1 INTRODUCTION

Information assets consist of sensitive and proprietary information, privacy-protected data, intellectual property, intangible assets, and information defined under international, federal, and state laws governing trade secrets, patents, and copyrights. Some specific information assets are scientific knowledge, branding, reputation, and business processes.

Information assets exist in many forms, including an individual's knowledge, spoken information, a process or procedure, information written on paper, an item (such as a model, prototype, device, or machine), data on an information technology (IT) or communications system, an electronic transmission, and data stored on electronic media (CD, DVD, magnetic tape, disc, memory card, thumb drive, volatile memory, etc.). The wide variety of forms enlarges the spectrum of protection approaches that must be considered.

This chapter addresses information asset protection (IAP), also known as information security or protection of proprietary information. The goal is to help the reader formulate an IAP program, implement a risk-based mitigation strategy, and identify protection gaps and solutions—all the while helping, not hindering the business or organization mission. As Richard Heffernan, former chairman of the ASIS Information Asset Protection Council, notes, "Assessing and addressing risks *enables* business."

1.2 HISTORY OF ESPIONAGE AND BUSINESS INTELLIGENCE COLLECTION

Throughout history, organizations have attempted to steal the information assets of other organizations. What is perhaps the earliest surviving record of espionage dates from about 1274 BC during Pharaoh Rameses' war with the Hittites (Crowdy, 2006, p. 15). Later, around 500 BC, the Chinese military strategist Sun Tzu wrote about five classes of spies: local spies, internal spies, converted spies, doomed spies, and surviving spies. He calls them "the sovereign's most precious faculty" (Sun Tzu, 1983, p. 78) and suggests that they can be used in settings beyond the battlefield, urging his readers to "[b]e subtle! and use your spies for every kind of business" (Sun Tzu, 1983, p. 81).

The historic silk trade between Asia and Europe provides a specific example of a failure of information asset protection. For years China had attempted to keep secret its techniques for raising silkworms and producing silk. In 552 AD the Byzantine emperor Justinian dispatched two monks to China to smuggle out silkworm eggs and mulberry tree seeds. As a result, China came to face significant competition in silk production.

Another example of intelligence collection involves Russia's Czar Peter the Great. In 1697-98, he traveled to the West to collect information on technology. With a team of military and industrial experts, he traveled to Poland, Germany, Holland, and England, studying gunnery, shipbuilding, seaport operations, Western culture, the scientific community, and the mint in England. By the early 1700s, Peter was employing much of the technology and business knowledge he had acquired. Years later, under other leadership, Russia used the military and economic power it gained under Peter the Great against western Europe.

One early example of U.S. industrial espionage involves Francis Cabot Lowell. In 1810, using a cover story that he was in Scotland for his health, Lowell "visited several [textile] mills normally closed to visitors, and with his photographic memory, was able to skirt British customs inspectors searching for stolen [loom] plans and blueprints. Back home, Lowell built his first textile plant in Waltham, Massachusetts, and America was well on its way into the industrial revolution" (Poteat, 2001). The Pinkerton National Detective Agency, founded in 1850, continued the U.S. trend by developing a business in intelligence and counter-intelligence.

Near the end of the nineteenth century, Frederick Taylor, considered the father of scientific management, also engaged in industrial espionage. He used several surreptitious techniques to research alleged patent violations:

- directing an agent to gain employment with a suspected company under false pretenses
- directing an agent to befriend employees of such a company to collect information on proprietary manufacturing processes

- directing an agent to establish a fake business arrangement with a company to learn details of its manufacturing process

- recruiting an employee of the company to provide information on manufacturing processes

- performing reverse engineering

Security Poster from the Manhattan Project Era

In the 1940s, U.S. nuclear weapons secrets were the target of many spies. Much was at stake: "Soviet espionage directed at the Manhattan Project probably hastened by at least 12–18 months the Soviet acquisition of the atomic bomb" (United States Department of Energy, 2007).

Throughout the Cold War, espionage flourished in both the national and commercial sectors. Much of the activity targeted dual-use technologies and information—those with both military and commercial applications. From the Western perspective, the predominant threat was that of the Soviet intelligence service, the KGB, and its military counterpart, the GRU. The KGB's Line X (Science and Technology Directorate) and its equivalent agencies in Eastern European states targeted dual-use technologies from private companies, government agencies, and universities.

In the 1970s, to mitigate the threats of espionage, open source collection, and aggressive targeting, the FBI established the Developing Espionage and Counterintelligence Awareness (DECA) Program, which aimed to educate U.S. industry—particularly cleared defense contractors—and solicit its support in reporting suspicious activities that might represent intelligence targeting. The DECA Program evolved into the Awareness of National Security Issues and Response (ANSIR) Program, and then the Counterintelligence Domain Program. Today it is known as the Counterintelligence Strategic Partnerships Program. These FBI liaison programs encourage outreach to the private sector and focus on protecting U.S. competitiveness by safeguarding the information assets of businesses.

A milestone in the fight to protect commercial and dual-use technologies in the United States was the enactment of the Economic Espionage Act (EEA) of 1996. The law made it a federal offense to steal trade secrets and gave the FBI the authority to investigate economic espionage. The law was crafted with input from ASIS International and its Safeguarding Proprietary Information Council, now the Information Asset Protection Council (http://www.asisonline.org/councils/SPI.xml).

Over the years, while the technologies employed in espionage have advanced tremendously, the general tactics and techniques have remained remarkably consistent. Even the approaches espoused by Sun Tzu and Frederick Taylor are still widely used today.

1.3 RISK MANAGEMENT APPROACH TO IAP

All organizations possess and use information assets that warrant protection. The nature of that protection should be based on a sound risk management approach.

The following is a risk assessment process for use in IAP:

- Identify information assets.
- Valuate information assets (assigning a quantitative value, such as dollars, or a qualitative value, such as high, medium, or low).
- Assess threats to information assets. Assess likely adversaries.
- Assess the likelihood of occurrence of threats.
- Identify existing and projected vulnerabilities.
- Assess the impact of a loss event or disclosure on the organization.
- Identify existing and planned security controls or other options for addressing risk.
- Assess and prioritize risks, based on their likelihood and organizational impact.

An information protection strategy should be designed to support the organization's goals, strategy, and timelines. As author Ira Winkler observes (2005, p. 35):

> Only when you understand the real components of risk can you put together an effective and appropriate strategy for protecting your organization and managing your risk. By addressing your vulnerabilities and *optimizing*, rather than *maximizing*, your counterespionage efforts, you can greatly improve your security.

> So the goal of your security program is to optimize risk, never minimize it. This is an extremely important distinction.

1.3.1 TODAY'S GLOBAL INFORMATION ENVIRONMENT

In terms of information exchange, the world is interconnected as never before. Because of this high—indeed global—level of interconnectedness, threats to information assets have become more diffuse and difficult to recognize, and they can act faster. The risk level is growing. As Michael D. Moberly, former chairman of the ASIS International Information Asset Protection Council, notes (2006):

> An unfortunate reality of international business transactions is that the probability that a company will … experience some form … of infringement, misappropriation, counterfeiting, or product piracy is growing.

Today, information assets that are compromised are almost always impossible to recall or contain in terms of dissemination (ASIS International, *Trends*, 2007, p. 41). They can be anywhere or everywhere in an instant.

The U.S. Office of the National Counterintelligence Executive, in its *Annual Report on Foreign Economic Collection and Industrial Espionage* (2006), recognized the challenges of the global information environment when it stated:

> Continued fierce global economic competition will fuel commercial technology theft … [and] illegal acquisitions of military and dual-use items … As globalization continues to pressure U.S. companies to move important technologies and even research and development facilities overseas, third-country venues may become increasingly important locations for U.S. technology acquisition. Both the security and legal frameworks for protecting technologies abroad tend to be weaker. …

1.3.2 THREAT CATEGORIES AND EXAMPLES

A key element of the risk assessment model is a thorough study of existing and projected threats. They may include intentional threats, natural threats, and inadvertent threats.

Intentional Threats

Historically, most attention has been focused on intentional threats. To assess them, one identifies potential adversaries and evaluates their capability and intention to target key information assets. It is important to think broadly when considering potential adversaries. Beside foreign and domestic competitors, adversaries may include foreign governments, activist groups, terrorist groups, criminal enterprises, information brokers, and vandals.

The FBI (2011) provides the following summary of today's threat environment:

> The Cold War is not over, it has merely moved into a new arena: the global marketplace. The FBI estimates that every year billions of U.S. dollars are lost to foreign and domestic competitors who deliberately target economic intelligence in flourishing U.S. industries and technologies, and who cull intelligence out of shelved technologies by exploiting open source information and company trade secrets. Foreign competitors who criminally seek economic intelligence generally operate in three ways:
>
> 1. They aggressively target and recruit insiders (often from the same national background) working for U.S. companies and research institutions;
>
> 2. They conduct economic intelligence through operations like bribery, cyber intrusions, theft, dumpster diving (in search of discarded intellectual property or prototypes), and wiretapping; and,
>
> 3. They establish seemingly innocent business relationships between foreign companies and U.S. industries to gather economic intelligence including trade secrets.

Research on adversaries' capabilities and intentions can be performed internally or by a trusted consultant or threat analysis firm.

Natural Threats

After natural disasters, many companies dissolve not because they lost their facilities but because they lost their information. In general, they did not have an effective preparedness plan (including off-site critical data backup and warm or hot sites) as part of a comprehensive business continuity plan. Often, the companies that fail are small, single-site companies without robust security and risk management functions. All entities, large and small, should prepare for natural threats that can severely affect their operations.

Inadvertent Threats

Perhaps the most frequently overlooked threats are inadvertent threats. These are also the most difficult to identify and evaluate, but they cannot be ignored. As Winkler (2005, pp. 53-54) observes:

> Although people want to hear about terrorists and hackers, the fact is that the largest losses are from the people in the mirror. … People make mistakes, and those mistakes are the most likely thing to hurt you … Human error and accidents … cause hundreds of billions of dollars [in losses] a year. When not appropriately anticipated, incidents can literally destroy a life or a company.

Inadvertent threats can be attributed to inadequate employee training, misunderstandings, lack of attention to detail, lax security enforcement, pressure to produce a deliverable, insufficient staffing, or other factors. It is thus essential to develop, promulgate, and enforce practical policies for IAP.

A few specific threats warrant mentioning because they are prevalent or represent a trend. The following issues should be considered, as appropriate, when conducting IAP risk assessments or developing mitigation strategies.

Data Mining

According to *Trends in Proprietary Information Loss* (ASIS International, 2007), the report of a survey by ASIS International, data mining (software-driven collection of open-source data and public information) has become a significant threat. Similarly, the Office of the National Counterintelligence Executive (2006) expresses the following concern for the future:

> The continued expansion of international linkages … will create global brokers skilled in moving technologies across borders and undercutting the ability … to control exports.

> [A] major concern is the fact that the nations best poised to use cybertools to access U.S. technologies are also the countries that traditionally have been the most aggressive.

Both governments and private sector entities are increasingly using automated tools to collect, filter, organize, analyze, and disseminate information. One result is the growth of information brokers. Another is the development of college courses, how-to books, and even "start your own home business" Web sites on the subject of data mining and information brokering. Of greater concern is that international terrorist groups are using data mining and advanced knowledge management techniques to support their intelligence gathering and attack planning activities.

Insiders

Trends in Proprietary Information Loss (ASIS International, 2007) found the exploitation of trusted relationships to be an increasing threat as well. Persons in such relationships include vendors, customers, joint venture partners, subcontractors, and outsourced providers. Likewise, a report for the Defense Personnel Security Research Center (Kramer, Heuer & Crawford, 2005) notes:

> Due to their knowledge of the public agencies and private companies that employ them, their familiarity with computer systems that contain classified and proprietary information, and their awareness of the value of protected information in the global market, insiders constitute a significant area of vulnerability for national security ...

> [T]he information revolution, global economic competition, the evolvement of new and nontraditional intelligence adversaries, and other changes in the domestic and international environment have converged to create unusually fertile ground for insider espionage. Primary findings of this research are as follows:

> - Technological advances in information storage and retrieval are dramatically improving insiders' ability to access and steal classified and proprietary information.

> - The global market for protected U.S. information is expanding. American insiders can sell more types of information to a broader range of foreign buyers than ever before.

> - The internationalization of science and commerce is placing more employees in a strategic position to establish contact with foreign scientists, businesspersons, and intelligence collectors, and to transfer scientific and technological material to them.

> - The increasing frequency of international travel is creating new opportunity for motivated sellers of information to establish contact with, and transfer information to, foreign entities. Foreign buyers have greater opportunity to contact and assess the vulnerabilities of American personnel with access to protected information.

> - Global Internet expansion is providing new opportunities for insider espionage. The Internet allows sellers and seekers of information to remain anonymous and provides means by which massive amounts of digitized material can be transmitted to foreign parties in a secure manner.

> - Americans are more vulnerable to experiencing severe financial crisis due to aggressive consumer spending habits and other factors. Financial problems are a common source of motivation for insider espionage.

- The increasing popularity of gambling and prevalence of gambling disorders suggests that greater numbers of insiders will commit workplace crimes such as espionage to pay off debts and to sustain gambling activities.

- Because organizational loyalty is diminishing, fewer employees may be deterred from committing espionage due to a sense of obligation to their employers. Changing conditions in the American workplace suggest that greater numbers of insiders may become motivated to steal information from employers to exact revenge for perceived mistreatment.

- More insiders now have ethnic ties to other countries, communicate with friends and family abroad, and interact with foreign businesspersons and governments. Foreign connections provide insiders with opportunities to transfer information outside the United States, and foreign ties can provide motivation for doing so.

- More Americans view human society as an evolving system of ethnically and ideologically diverse, interdependent persons and groups. While this is beneficial in many respects, it is also possible that some insiders with a global orientation to world affairs will, under extreme circumstances, view espionage as morally justifiable if they feel that sharing information will benefit the world community.

A study of 49 insider incidents found the following (United States Secret Service, 2005, pp. 11-16):

- Of the perpetrators, 59 percent were former employees or contractors of the affected organization while 41 percent were current employees or contractors.

- Perpetrator age ranged from 17 to 60 years.

- Three out of ten perpetrators had a previous arrest record.

- A negative work-related event triggered the action in almost all the cases.

- In 80 percent of the cases, the perpetrator came to the attention of management due to inappropriate behaviors before the incident (e.g., tardiness, truancy, arguments with coworkers, or poor job performance).

- In 31 percent of the cases, others had information about the perpetrator's plan to cause harm; a direct threat was made in 20 percent of the incidents.

Counterfeiting and Piracy

From blue jeans and purses to chemicals and pharmaceuticals, counterfeiting and piracy are growing problems with both economic and safety implications. In a recent statement, the United States General Accountability Office (2007) stated that

> government efforts to protect and enforce intellectual property (IP) rights domestically and overseas are crucial to preventing billions of dollars in losses to U.S. industry and IP rights owners and to avoiding health and safety risks resulting from the trade in counterfeit and pirated goods.

The threat of counterfeiting and piracy is particularly consequential for small businesses, which are increasingly entering the global marketplace and operating internationally. As Moberly (2006) observes:

> Startups, early stage firms, and small and medium size companies that are rich in intangible assets often do not recognize the scope or the economic impact of counterfeiting and piracy, globally. Nor do they seem to realize how reactive most conventional defenses (i.e., patents, copyrights, trademarks) are against nanosecond piracy and counterfeiting.

1.3.3 RISK ASSESSMENT AND DUE DILIGENCE

It is sometimes said in the business world that "you can't manage it if you can't measure it." Risk assessments should identify risks, quantify them, and prioritize them according to the organization's criteria for risk acceptance. The results of the assessment should help in selecting and prioritizing actions for managing risks.

Assessments should be performed regularly and should include risk monitoring to address changes in security requirements as well as changes in the nature of the information assets, threats, frequency of threat occurrence, vulnerabilities, and impacts. In addition, monitoring helps in evaluating the effectiveness of security and other risk mitigation measures.

1.3.4 ATTAINING BUY-IN

Executive buy-in is essential to IAP. Because information, intangible assets, and intellectual property are integral to almost any organization, one might expect it to be easy to convince executives to embrace and support an information asset protection program. However, gaining such a commitment is often difficult because of the intangible nature of the assets. Therefore, IAP professionals should strive to make a convincing business case for proactive strategies, the dedication of resources, and the ability to make inputs to the business decision making process—in other words, to get a seat at the table.

One step toward this end is to articulate the business impacts of a loss event. According to *Trends in Proprietary Information Loss* (ASIS International, 2007), the top business impacts are as follows:

- loss of company reputation/image/goodwill
- loss of competitive advantage in one product/service
- reduced projected/anticipated returns or profitability
- loss of core business technology or process
- loss of competitive advantage in multiple products/services

Other impacts of proprietary information loss include loss of use, ownership, or control of intellectual property rights, as well as loss of proprietary information or prototypes that would facilitate product counterfeiting.

Security management personnel can also point out that IAP benefits the business because it does the following (Moberly, 2007):

- enhances fiduciary oversight, control, and stewardship of key intangible assets

- aligns information assets with business operations and the organization's strategic vision

- allows more efficient allocation of traditional and IT security resources

- allows more timely pursuit of information asset compromises and intellectual property rights (IPR) violations

- serves as leverage in negotiating coverage and premiums for intellectual property (IP) and information technology (IT) insurance

- provides consistency in regulatory reporting of intangible assets

- standardizes internal and external handling of intangible assets

- identifies key internal and external sources of intangible assets and intellectual capital

Other approaches suggested by Moberly include the use of quantitative methods by IAP professionals wherever possible and assuming the role of a business resource (an enabler, not an impediment) for the enterprise. Ultimately, the responsibility for protecting information assets rests with the leadership of an organization.

Mid-level managers, too, must be won over if an IAP program is to succeed (Winkler, 2005):

> Gaining the support of first- and second-tier management is critical. The managers who see the employees every day are the ones who will actually be there to notice when people are following security practices and when they are not. These are the folks who can influence security the most.

Finally, the IAP program must be embraced by every other individual—inside or outside the company—who has access to the company's information assets.

1.4 APPROACHES TO RISK MITIGATION

Much of the following content is from the ASIS International *Information Asset Protection Guideline* (2007).

1.4.1 BASIC PROTECTION PRACTICES

The FBI (2011) lists the following steps for protecting a business from espionage:

- Recognize there is an insider and outsider threat to your company.

- Identify and valuate trade secrets.

- Implement a proactive plan for safeguarding trade secrets.

- Secure physical and electronic versions of your trade secrets.

- Confine intellectual knowledge on a "need-to-know" basis.

- Provide training to employees about your company's intellectual property plan and security.

The measures that follow are consistent with the FBI approach. Most can be applied to any private or public organization.

IAP Policies and Awareness

Clear, practical, and well-promulgated policies strengthen any security program. In developing a policy, several steps are vital:

- The organization's leadership should show its commitment to IAP by providing appropriate resources and requiring all business units to develop strategies to align business and protection goals.

- A dedicated department, group, or individuals should be tasked with policy management and auditing.

- All business units, personnel, temporary employees, vendors, consultants, contractors, and business partners should be required to adhere to the policy.

- IAP training should be delivered repeatedly at new employee orientation sessions; during inspections, all-hands conferences, and visits to other facilities; on the company intranet; in newsletters; and as part of IT or human resources training.

- IAP awareness and training efforts should be documented.

It is important to identify what information should be protected and when, and then identify the many forms this information may take over its life cycle. Only a certain segment of the organization's information may warrant protection. Once such information is identified, it should be classified so the most significant information assets will receive the greatest degree of protection.

The policy statement sets the tone for the organization and, if enforced, may support legal actions if they become necessary. The policy should clarify that information is one of the organization's most important resources, that all information needs to be appropriately evaluated for sensitivity, and that protection measures must be sufficient to ensure confidentiality, integrity, availability, accountability, recoverability, auditability, and non-repudiation of information in both the physical and cyber environment. Random audits should be conducted to ensure compliance with IAP policy.

A sample IAP policy statement is provided in Appendix A.

Identification and Marking of Protected Information

Information warranting protection must be appropriately identified and marked. Various levels are used to distinguish the degree of sensitivity or the degree of protection warranted: confidential, restricted, limited, non-public, etc. Most organizations use two to four levels of sensitivity.

For example, many businesses divide information in three categories: approved for external release (unrestricted access), internal (limited to employees and contractors), and confidential (limited by a specific need to know). Information may be in electronic, oral, written, or other forms. Whenever practical, the material should be marked or tagged. The originator of the information typically determines the classification level, and authorized users may not disclose contents without the owner's approval.

Access to internal information should be restricted to company personnel or others who have signed a nondisclosure agreement. Standards for granting access may also include a satisfactory background investigation. An employee's access should be based on his or her current job function and need to know, not solely on position or management level.

1.4.2 PHYSICAL SECURITY

IAP professionals should coordinate closely with physical security staff to harmonize protective efforts in several categories.

Layered Protection (Defense in Depth)

This concept, which applies a vision of concentric rings or layers of protection to any asset, is most commonly thought of in terms of physical security. The same approach, however, should be employed in protecting sensitive information assets. Defense in depth can be viewed from three different perspectives, in which the concentric rings or layers of protection represent the following:

- Increasing levels of trust for those who are given access to successive layers. For example, a member of the maintenance staff will likely have a lower level of trust (and therefore access) than the director of research and development for the company. Based on their respective levels of trust, they each would have appropriate but different levels of access to information or facilities.

- Different security technologies or measures that operate in concert. By applying overlapping and diverse security technologies and measures, security staff can identify and fill any gaps in protective coverage. Benefits must be weighed against costs.

- Successive layers employed to delay, detect, and deter intruders. Each successive layer of protection may further delay an adversary, offer an additional opportunity to detect the intrusion, and deter an adversary from advancing.

These perspectives apply equally to automated systems protection and to information in other forms (hard copy, process, knowledge, intangible, etc.).

To implement layered protection, an IAP professional should do the following:

- Apply multiple levels or layers of protective measures to critical information assets appropriate to their sensitivity or exposure to loss.

- Ensure that successive levels or layers of protective measures complement rather than conflict with each other.

- Build a coordinated strategy that integrates different families of protective measures, such as physical security, personnel security, technical security, access control, education and awareness, and policies and procedures.

Normally, facilities and systems housing company information should be afforded protection from unauthorized entry at all times. Access to internal or confidential information should require authentication via presentation of unique, preauthorized physical and logical access credentials. The level of access granted should be consistent with the level of information a person needs for work.

Handling of Documents and Records

These functions represent the everyday management of sensitive information in paper or electronic form. The following protective steps are recommended:

- Place shredders or secure collection receptacles near printers, copiers, and fax machines.

- Place signs in such areas to remind employees that overruns and misprints must be destroyed.

- Where appropriate, document any transfers (internal and external) of sensitive records or documents.

- Carefully select any contractors that destroy records, documents, or sensitive information.

- Destroy records and sensitive information in a manner that precludes reconstruction consistent with its level of sensitivity, and document the date and place of destruction.

- Destroy obsolete records regularly, according to a record retention schedule.

- Destroy incidental and duplicate records on a regular basis.

- Store media awaiting destruction in secure containers.

- If possible, avoid discarding destroyed media in trash receptacles accessible to the public.

- When records and information are being transported, protect them with locked containers, seals, escorts, radio frequency identification tags, transportation logs, and other means.

Appendix E presents more information on document disposal and destruction.

Protection of Information in Physical Form

- Prototypes and models

  - These should be afforded all the same physical security, access controls, classification, employee vetting, verification, and documentation as other information assets. They may exist in the form of paper designs, hardware, test vehicles, market test materials, software, or other prototypes.

  - Obsolete prototypes, models, and test items should be destroyed so they cannot be reversed engineered.

  - Contractors or vendors entrusted with prototypes, models, or test items should be contractually bound to protect them according to the owner's policies and procedures. Also, they should be given instructions for return or disposition of the items when no longer needed.

- Manufacturing processes and equipment

  - Access to production or processing facilities should be restricted to employees who require access to carry out their responsibilities.

  - Photography in production or processing areas should be restricted.

  - Contractors with access to the production or processing area should have executed nondisclosure agreements such as those required for handling other sensitive information.

- Employees, contractors, and visitors entering the production or processing area should display identification badges indicating their status and approved level of access. In addition, visitors should be required to sign in using an automated visitor control system or visitor log.

- Obsolete or damaged production equipment, as well as scrap, should be disposed of in a manner that does not compromise or divulge information regarding the production or processing area.

- Information regarding loading dock activity (such as materials and quantities received in shipments) may also require protection.

- Compartmentalization and physical or visual barriers

    - Information of various classifications should stored separately.

    - Safeguards such as barriers and covers should be used when sensitive information may be exposed to view by unauthorized individuals.

1.4.3 PERSONNEL SECURITY

Personnel security plays a key role in IAP. It includes such matters as due diligence investigations of potential partners, standard preemployment screening, and vetting of subcontractors, vendors, and consultants.

The screening process often is outside the control of the security, risk management, or IAP functions and may instead be handled by the legal or human resources departments. An additional challenge is that these investigations often require long lead times. Therefore, the procedures are sometimes circumvented, possibly putting information assets at greater risk.

To overcome these challenges, the IAP professional should establish an effective communications channel with other organizational elements involved in these screening functions; ensure that vetting covers all potential trusted parties with whom protected information may be shared; and periodically review personnel screening, due diligence, and vetting procedures.

1.4.4 PRIVACY PROTECTION

All organizations handle private information pertaining to their employees, management, relationships, customers, or others. In some organizations this includes information which is designated as "Personally Identifiable Information" or "PII." To maintain trust and meet legal requirements, IAP professionals should do the following:

- Establish specific privacy policies and designate an employee responsible for implementing and managing the privacy program.

- Evaluate privacy information relating to employees, partners, vendors, customers, and others and determine legal and regulatory requirements.

- Ensure systems are in place to guard employee and customer privacy.

- Provide a mechanism to investigate compromises of privacy information (including identity theft) and report the incidents to affected individuals or organizations (victims) as appropriate.

- Review applicable federal, state, and international guidelines, such as those shown at the U.S. Federal Trade Commission site (www.ftc.gov/privacy) and in various European Union data protection directives to ensure full compliance with applicable laws and regulations.

- Clearly mark privacy information to state how the information will be used and made available to others, what notifications and actions will be taken if a compromise occurs, and instructions for destruction or disposition when the information is no longer needed.

- Conduct program audits to ensure privacy policies are properly implemented.

1.4.5 **BUSINESS PRACTICES**

ASIS International holds that security is a business function. Thus, IAP principles should be incorporated into the business's everyday practices and culture. Conversely, key aspects of the organization's mission and business philosophy should be included in the IAP strategy. The following are some steps for harmonizing IAP and general business practices:

- Coordinate IAP matters with all appropriate elements of the company: legal, human resources, security, risk management, safety, IT, research and development, contracting, marketing, public relations, training, logistics, competitive intelligence, international relations, accounting and finance, facilities, and others.

- Incorporate IAP into the organization's business continuity plan to ensure that critical information retains its availability, confidentiality, and integrity during all phases of crisis situations including response and recovery.

- Infuse IAP-related material into employee training and professional development programs.

- Communicate IAP issues to all levels of management.

One business activity that raises special risks to a company's information is the establishment of relationships (such as partnerships or outsourcing agreements) with other companies, domestically or internationally. In those relationships, companies may inadvertently let down their guard with respect to information protection. In the United States, thousands of front companies have been established, often by foreign governments, to collect information from U.S. businesses. Therefore, it is essential to conduct due diligence investigations before partnering with—and sharing information with—other companies.

1.4.6 **OPERATIONS SECURITY OR INFORMATION RISK MANAGEMENT**

Operations security (OPSEC) is a protection approach developed in the military to protect unclassified information that could reveal sensitive plans and operations. In 1988 in the United States, a National Security Decision Directive instituted OPSEC throughout the executive branch of the federal government. Since then, it has been successfully applied to the protection of sensitive research and development information, technical data, product test data, law enforcement sensitive information, and commercial information from competitive intelligence efforts.

In effect, OPSEC is a system of "information risk management" and is sometimes called by that name in the private sector. It calls for viewing the big picture and identifying any protection gaps that remain despite current security measures. Those gaps represent avenues by which information assets could be compromised, either intentionally or inadvertently. Gaps may exist, for example, between legal and security strategies or between protection measures in different countries. OPSEC or information risk management should be practiced in organizations of all sizes, but it is particularly valuable for smaller businesses that may not have a large security or IAP staff or a great deal of security resources (Peterson, 2005).

OPSEC responds to the fact that small bits of information taken from several different sources can be combined to reveal sensitive information. The following steps may help organizations prevent the release of those small but combinable bits of information:

- Develop specific, tailored IAP policies for key projects.

- Ensure that peripheral information (such as supply orders or hiring plans), facility enhancements and other observable activities, and other indicators do not provide valuable intelligence to a competitor or adversary.

- Consider the vulnerability of information released to outside entities as part of joint ventures or trusted partner (vendor, supplier, client) arrangements. The other entity may not have sufficient IAP measures in place.

- Examine the company's publicly available information to determine whether, in the aggregate, it reveals sensitive information. Periodically review the company's Web site and the sites of any partners.

- Assess vulnerabilities by taking the adversary's perspective. Defend against realistic collection techniques.

- Implement an approval process for any presentations, papers, or articles that may contain information pertinent to sensitive activities or plans.

1.4.7 **TRAVEL AND MEETING SECURITY**

Sensitive information may be particularly vulnerable when employees travel, attend trade shows, and participate in on- or off-site meetings.

Domestic and International Travel

Special circumstances, threats, and vulnerabilities may arise during business travel. Business travelers with any form of sensitive information can do the following to reduce the risk to that information:

- Obtain a pre-travel security briefing or consult travel advisories, notifications, information services, and publications prior to departure. The U.S. Department of State's Overseas Security Advisory Council (OSAC) is one source of such information.

- Keep a low profile to minimize targeting. Avoid using items that visibly divulge the traveler's employer or personal or national identity.

- Restrict information carried to what is absolutely necessary.

- Carry information on one's person, not in checked baggage, and do not surrender baggage containing sensitive information to baggage handlers or bellmen.

- Be aware of the risk of technical surveillance (electronic eavesdropping).

- Avoid working on or discussing sensitive information in public areas or on public transportation.

- Use computer privacy screens, cable locks, and other measures to protect information on computers.

- Avoid the use of hotel fax machines, copy facilities, and business centers for sensitive information.

- If it is necessary to transfer electronic files to someone else's computer to facilitate printing, copying, or projection, be sure to delete those files and any temporary files afterward.

- Report actual, attempted, or suspected targeting of information during travel.

Trade Shows

Trade shows are a traditional venue for business and government intelligence collection. The U.S. Office of the National Counterintelligence Executive (2006) calls conventions and expositions a particular threat:

> [T]hese visits continued to yield useful information for collectors. Conventions, expositions, and seminars offered rich collection and targeting opportunities for foreign entities because they directly linked foreign experts with U.S. specialists, programs, and technologies. Furthermore, these venues gave foreign specialists the opportunity to compare and contrast the various technologies and to ask technical questions to fill intelligence gaps.

The following steps may help:

- Establish an IAP awareness program and reporting mechanism tailored to individuals who travel to trade shows, conferences, symposia, and technical meetings. The program should address elicitation techniques, among other topics, and remind travelers of any nondisclosure agreements.

- Identify high-risk travelers based on their position, project, access, or clearance within the company. Develop special procedures for such travelers.

- Consider documenting all information and equipment (such as notebook computers or handheld devices) to be carried to the meeting. If appropriate, make backup copies of the information.

- Debrief travelers on their return when appropriate (e.g., for high-risk travelers or travelers attending technical conferences abroad).

On- and Off-Site Meetings

On- and off-site meetings, especially those of a business or scientific nature, have a long history of being targeted for information collection and development of relationships with attendees. The following steps may help IAP professionals reduce the risk such meetings pose:

- Obtain an annual schedule of the organization's strategic and critical business meetings and develop an IAP strategy for each meeting as necessary, based on risk assessment.

- Before a venue is confirmed, obtain floor plans and details concerning the site's telecommunications and audiovisual infrastructure.

- Encourage meeting planners to select sites and rooms based on information protection concerns.

- Arrange for a low-profile event when appropriate, minimizing signage and electronic postings of events, sponsors, room locations, and schedules. Use meeting names that do not suggest the subject matter or identify attendees.

- Determine the need to perform a technical surveillance countermeasures inspection before and during meetings. Vulnerabilities may include unencrypted wireless mikes, wireless headsets, audio leakage, electronic equipment brought by participants or others, and unsecured telecommunications equipment, cables, and terminals.

- Determine the need for secure shipment and storage before, during, and after the event.

- Maintain security of printed materials and computer media during reproduction, transportation, and storage.

- Minimize the distribution of hard copy information.

- Ensure that electronic presentations are protected during creation, editing, transmission, and presentation. Also, ensure that they are completely removed from any computers used for presentation that are not owned by the company.

- Ensure that suppliers follow appropriate information security practices.

- Make arrangements for limiting access to meetings rooms. If appropriate, use security officers to provide 24-hour security of meeting rooms and electronic equipment, including laptops.

- Collect information and notes left behind by attendees. Arrange for secure disposal.

1.4.8 PREVENTING AND DETECTING COUNTERFEITING AND ILLEGAL COPYING

The following steps may help IAP professionals prevent and detect counterfeiting and illegal copying:

- Monitor the Internet to identify counterfeit products.

- Train employees to watch for counterfeit products and known suspects, competitors, or common schemes.

- Require all employees, vendors, and subcontractors to sign nondisclosure agreements (NDAs).

- Employ anti-counterfeiting technology.

- Number all technical memoranda and reports.

- Conduct regular compliance and inventory control audits, inside and outside the organization.

- Work with law enforcement and prosecutorial agencies on detection, awareness, alerts, and information sharing.

- Consider participating in the U.S. Customs and Border Protection (CBP) Intellectual Property Rights e-Recordation program (https://apps.cbp.gov/e-recordations). Under the program, IP owners can record their copyrights and trademarks though an electronic registration process. This recordation program allows CBP to stop any registered products suspected of being in violation of U.S. copyright or trademark laws, and to notify the asset owner.

1.5 **LEGAL PROTECTIONS**

Privacy-protected information is specifically regulated by the Health Insurance Portability and Accountability Act (HIPAA), the Privacy Act, and the Financial Services Modernization Act (Gramm-Leach-Bliley Act) in the United States; by the Data Protection Directive in the European Union; and by other laws and regulations worldwide.[1] All successful IAP programs assign a specialist the responsibility of monitoring pending legislation and regulations related to the protection of information assets. It is very important to assess any potential effects those changes may have on the organization.

Listed below are matters to discuss with the organization's legal counsel:

- taking enforcement actions on any patent, copyright, or trademark/service mark violations

- understanding current legal protocols and case law to assist in determining lost profits and financial damages and ascertaining appropriate protection strategies

- understanding the status of intellectual property rights protection and the nature of violations in each jurisdiction where the organization plans to do business

In addition, information asset owners must recognize that legal protections are effective only if the owner is willing to pursue recourse when a violation occurs. This activity can consume an enormous amount of time and financial resources. Asset owners should consider, in advance, their intended approach to resolving violations when they occur.

According to the United States Patent and Trademark Office (2007), a patent is a property right granted to an inventor to exclude others from making, using, offering for sale, or selling the invention for a limited time; a trademark consists of words, names, symbols, devices, or images applied to products or used in connection with goods or services to identify their source; and a copyright is used to protect the expression of ideas in literary, artistic, and musical works.

The best way to start addressing infringement of patents, copyrights, and trademarks is to register those rights. It is the intellectual property owner's responsibility to understand and comply with the requirements related to protecting those rights in each relevant jurisdiction. It is important to seek expert help when registering patents, trademarks, and copyrights and when addressing potential infringement. Membership in anti-counterfeiting organizations can also be helpful.

---

[1]   For more on automated information regulations, see the *Regulatory Compliance Planning Guide* at http://www.microsoft.com/technet/security/guidance/complianceandpolicies/compliance/rcguide/default.mspx?mfr=true.

The U.S. State Department provides guidance on intellectual property rights issues in many countries, typically listed under "IPR Tool Kit" on the specific embassy Web site. For example, intellectual property rights issues in China are discussed at http://beijing. usembassychina.org.cn/ipr.html.

1.5.1 COPYRIGHTS

Under international law, copyrights do not have to be registered to be protected. Nevertheless, an author or copyright holder can formalize ownership through government registration, which may help in any later enforcement actions.

The copyright owner should not allow control of the copyright to fall into the hands of the organization's agents or distributors. It is important to do the following:

- Incorporate copyright protections into contracts and marketing strategies.

- Enter into written, enforceable contracts that require agents, suppliers, distributors, and employees to protect the copyright.

- Refuse to assign or license the copyright until all consequences are fully understood.

- Ensure that the copyright remains with the organization upon termination of the assignment, license, transaction, or investment.

If an organization discovers that its copyright has been violated, it is essential to take action immediately. Response tools include

- hiring legal counsel;

- informing the proper authorities;

- conducting investigations, raids, and seizures; and

- initiating civil litigation, administrative proceedings, and criminal prosecutions.

In deciding which tools to use, it helps to ask the following questions:

- Is the copyright registered or otherwise protectable in the particular country?

- Is the harm being caused in that country or overseas?

- What is the source of the harm: competitors, employees, agents, or contractors?

1.5.2 **TRADEMARKS, TRADE DRESS, AND SERVICE MARKS**

New market entrants should develop a strategy for protecting their company's intellectual property early in the planning stages of doing business in any country. Registration of trademarks before the product enters the stream of commerce in any country is the primary means of ensuring that the mark is eligible for protection under that country's law and ensuring that trademark infringement can be remedied through administrative or judicial proceedings. It is also important to apply appropriate trade or service markings and notices to materials produced by the company.

When doing business outside the organization's home country, the best weapon is prevention. The following are some practical steps:

- Become familiar with the organization's rights before the product crosses the border.

- Develop and register a host country language version. Otherwise, the market may do so, creating a nickname for the product. The company may not like that name, or someone else in that country may register it, forcing the company to buy the rights to it.

- Register the trademark in neighboring countries to provide protection for potential expansion and to block others from registering marks on products that consumers may confuse with the company's.

- Conduct ongoing research to identify products that infringe the trademark or that bear a trademark confusingly similar to the company's but registered by another party.

1.5.3 **PATENTS**

An inventor may protect an invention by patenting it or by deeming it a trade secret. Patents convey a range of benefits but require that the inventor publicly disclose the invention's elements, and a patent lasts only 20 years. By contrast, a trade secret is not disclosed and may last indefinitely. In addition, while stealing a trade secret may violate criminal laws, there are no criminal laws regarding patent infringement (United States Department of Justice, 2006). The following is one approach for protecting inventions:

- Follow trade secret guidelines for all newly discovered processes or products until a patent has been issued.

- Ensure that patent protection is acquired in all appropriate jurisdictions.

- Consider using the U.S. International Trade Commission as a venue for resolving patent disputes.

1.5.4 **TRADE SECRETS**

Trade secrets need not be registered with any outside agency, so the owner can maintain a greater degree of control over the asset. For information to be considered a trade secret, the owner must be able to prove that the information added value or benefit to the owner, the trade secret was specifically identified, and the owner provided a reasonable level of protection for the trade secret. The term "reasonable" carries a high standard; the owner must demonstrate a robust security program and strict protection measures that are clearly and consistently defined, communicated, and enforced.

The following steps should help the organization protect its trade secrets:

- Document the identification and valuation of the trade secrets, their role in establishing competitive advantage in the industry, and the full scope of protection measures instituted to protect them.

- Ensure that reasonable traditional and cyber security measures are in place to prevent unauthorized access to the trade secrets.

- Conduct periodic, random security audits to ensure compliance.

- Execute nondisclosure agreements with employees, suppliers, consultants, and others before any disclosure.

- Establish need-to-know criteria to ensure that individuals have access to only the specific information they need to do their jobs.

- Institute effective information warning notifications to ensure that individuals are aware of exactly what needs to be protected.

- Take steps to properly destroy materials no longer needed.

1.5.5 **INTERNATIONAL CONCERNS**

A company planning to introduce intellectual property into another country should begin working with lawyers well in advance, and those lawyers should have experience in the anticipated market. The company should also inventory its intellectual property and other sensitive information and develop plans for protecting each type of information.

In addition to applying for patents, assigning any patent rights, and licensing technology as appropriate, companies should evaluate the risks posed by contractual relationships. Many intellectual property disputes arise between companies doing business together. Companies should use nondisclosure agreements in negotiations and contracts, identify and restrict disclosure of all technical data only to those who have a need to know, and compartmentalize knowledge. Some forms of information, such as tools, dies, or formulas, can be protected through traditional physical security measures.

The company should also conduct an intellectual property due-diligence investigation, reviewing the market of the country under consideration for existing infringements of the company's rights and studying the experiences of similar companies in that country. Moreover, the company should become familiar with the country's intellectual property rules and regulations. Licensors should consult qualified counsel to determine how much of a license must be recorded to ensure that the licensor's rights are not compromised.

An excellent source for advice on doing business abroad is the U.S. State Department's Overseas Security Advisory Council (OSAC). Its Web site (www.osac.gov) provides a variety of useful documents, including Security Guidelines for American Enterprises Abroad. OSAC also offers country-specific advice on intellectual property laws and regulations, as well as information on trends in infringement.

1.5.6 NONDISCLOSURE AGREEMENTS AND CONTRACTS

Written nondisclosure agreements (NDAs) ensure a common understanding and a legal obligation regarding the protection of information assets. NDAs should acknowledge that any information on any medium that records business communications or transactions is considered an official record under the law and will be handled according to the policies and procedures regarding information assets. Confidentiality obligations may need to be extended to board members, employees, agents, and others.

All employees should execute an NDA as a condition of employment. Via the agreement, they should acknowledge that all information assets regarding the employer, vendors, and customers are considered confidential, will be kept confidential, and are the property of the employer. Employee NDAs should also include verification that the employee has read, understands, and will abide by the IAP policies and procedures. When their employment ends, employees should be reminded of their continuing obligations under the NDA.

Similarly, a contractor, subcontractor, consultant, or vendor with access to information assets should be contractually bound to protect the information to the same degree as it is protected in-house.

Sample NDAs are provided in Appendix C.

1.6 TECHNICAL PROTECTIVE MEASURES

This section addresses means of mitigating technical collection threats. Incorporating traditional protection measures with these technical approaches represents an application of convergence in asset protection. Many of the approaches described here require specialized expertise, and some services may need to be outsourced. It is essential to select outsourcing partners carefully, as they will necessarily gain access to sensitive information.

1.6.1 TECHNICAL SURVEILLANCE COUNTERMEASURES

Technical surveillance countermeasures (TSCM) are services, equipment, and techniques designed to locate, identify, and neutralize technical surveillance activities (electronic eavesdropping). TSCM should be part of an organization's overall protection strategy.

As part of the TSCM effort, IAP professionals should arrange for regular inspection of telecommunications equipment, cables, and terminals using equipment, methods, and personnel capable of detecting current threats. Offices and meeting rooms should be inspected for technical surveillance vulnerabilities regularly and randomly and also immediately before any sensitive discussions.

1.6.2 PROTECTION IN AN IT ENVIRONMENT

This section presents highlights of IT security issues relevant to IAP programs. IT security is covered in greater detail elsewhere in the *Protection of Assets*.

Because much information exists in electronic form, IAP professionals must consider protection of both networks (wired and wireless) and stand-alone computers. Most effective is a layered approach that integrates physical, procedural, and logical protection measures. The following are some recommended steps:

- Change default passwords, user names, and administrative accounts.

- Assign administrative privileges appropriately. Administrators should use non-privileged accounts when not performing system administration.

- Limit and monitor physical access to network components.

- Ensure a separation of duties for IT staff where possible.

- Install and update antivirus and firewall software on network servers and client devices (laptops, workstations, and personal electronic devices). Firewalls can protect information from external and internal intrusions.

- Implement formal patch management and configuration management protocols.

- Train users in computer security awareness, including the risks associated with remote access, mobile access, and wireless technology.

- Require external organizations with access to the company's information systems to maintain an equivalent security posture.

An intrusion detection system (IDS) monitors for malicious programs and unauthorized changes to files and settings. They also monitor network traffic and provide alarms for network-based attacks. For some environments, an intrusion prevention system should be considered, especially where staff might not be available to actively monitor or act on alerts from the IDS. Additionally, extrusion prevention systems can be configured to prevent the unauthorized exit of information.

Special attention should also be given to the protection of data and access control in cloud computing environments and/or where third parties have some legitimate access to computing resources or information content. This also applies where an organization employs an on-line backup, data warehousing, or records archiving vendor.

IAP professionals should also be aware of the following:

- **Logical network access control.** This the process by which users are identified and granted privileges to information, systems, or resources.

- **Application security.** Modern business applications typically consist of custom code, third-party software, and one or more servers. Improper integration of these components can result in a vulnerability that can later be exploited to gain unauthorized access to data.

- **Sanitizing information systems and media.** Sanitizing is the process of removing data on a storage medium (such as a hard drive) before the medium is reused. Methods include overwriting and degaussing (magnetic erasure). An alternative is physical destruction.

- **Encryption.** Encryption obscuring the meaning of information by altering or encoding it in such a way that it can only be decoded by people for whom it is intended.

- **Digital signature.** This authenticates the identity of the sender of a message. Digital signatures are especially important for electronic commerce and e-mail.

- **Wireless environment.** Wireless local area networks (WLANs) are convenient but can introduce risks. They are generally considered less secure than wired LANs, so the types of data transported by them should be carefully evaluated.

1.6.3 **PROTECTION IN SPECIAL ENVIRONMENTS**

Several environments pose special requirements for information asset protection.

Cell Phones, Laptops, and Personal Digital Assistants (PDAs)

Handheld or mobile devices often are not protected by the IT security infrastructure of the company or the physical security of an enclosed facility. People often fail to recognize the amount and significance of the data stored and communicated on such devices. The following steps can improve the security of portable devices:

- Require employees to acknowledge, in writing, that company-issued equipment and any information produced or stored on it are the property of the employer.

- Control and discourage the use of mobile devices with embedded cameras, particularly around sensitive materials or in restricted areas.

- Do not store social security numbers, credit card numbers, or passwords on wireless devices.

- Lock cell phones when they are not in use.

- Consider installing software that can remotely lock a phone or erase its data if the phone is lost or stolen.

- Tag or engrave laptops with the organization's name, address, and phone number to increase the odds of recovering lost items.

- Prevent the last logged-in user name from being displayed.

- Use a nondescript carrying case.

- Be careful when using a wireless hot spot (such as in a hotel or airport). There is a risk of logging onto a nearby computer that may be used for identity theft.

- Configure laptops not to auto-connect to wireless access points listed as unsecure.

- Regularly check with the device manufacturer for software updates or news of security vulnerabilities.

E-Conferencing

Meetings via video, telephone, and Web-based technology are convenient but not necessarily secure. The IAP professional should find out how a service provider protects private information. It is also important to find out the provider's policy regarding passwords. Whenever possible, encryption should be used for the transfer of data.

Unless the security measures can be validated, users should assume their discussions are not private.

Outsourcing

Outsourcing transfers operational control and accountability to outside parties and may increase the risk to information assets. In certain cases, the information risks are not easily identifiable and may result from subtle or hidden clauses in contracts. Due diligence should be performed for potential providers. The following are some suggested steps:

- Look into the provider's financial performance and reputation, including intellectual property rights violations, trade complaints, export control issues, links to foreign governments, and links to suspect firms.

- Establish individual and corporate nondisclosure agreements with providers and their subcontractors.

- Conduct on-site security reviews of the provider before signing an outsourcing agreement and regularly thereafter.

- Identify, physically and logically, where outsource personnel will work and ensure that appropriate physical security and information technology measures are in place.

- Consult with legal counsel on laws and regulations (of all participating countries) on the export and import of technology, personal and privacy information, and implementation of protection procedures to help ensure compliance.

1.7 RESPONSE AND RECOVERY AFTER AN INFORMATION LOSS

The following are key steps to take after an information loss:

Investigation

- Thoroughly investigate known and suspected compromises of information to support law enforcement, litigation, asset recovery, identification of the root cause of the incident, prevention of future incidents, and loss or damage assessment.

- Establish an investigative plan and coordinate with counsel.

- Identify investigative resources that are required from internal or external sources.

- Establish and maintain liaison with law enforcement and investigative service providers as well as various information sources.

Damage Assessment

- As quickly and completely as possible, determine what information was compromised.

- Determine the implications of the compromise in terms of economic loss, project delays, operational impact, corporate image, shareholder confidence, legal liability, and corporate relationships (with partners, vendors, suppliers, subcontractors, etc.).

- Report the actual and potential impacts to an appropriate level of management.

Recovery and Follow-up

- Realize that the two primary elements of recovery are (1) to return to normal business operations as soon as possible and (2) to implement measures to prevent a recurrence of the problem.

- Implement any applicable portions of the organization's business continuity plan.

- Conduct a root cause analysis and implement corrective actions based on its findings. Maintain a database of incidents (including allegations and suspected incidents) to support root cause analysis and analyze any trends.

1.8 SUMMARY

In protecting information assets, an effective protection strategy begins with a clear, practical policy that is shared with all relevant parties and is fairly enforced. The right mix of protection measures varies for each organization. Typically, an organization will need to employ both security measures (personnel, equipment, awareness training) and legal measures (copyrights, patents, trademarks, nondisclosure agreements, contract clauses) to protect its information assets.

An IAP program should strive for prevention of information loss, but must also be prepared for response to losses that do occur, and recovery from a loss event involving information assets. Finally, for pervasive risk management, the IAP program should be developed in parallel with major business operations and business continuity planning to ensure consistent and well-orchestrated protection strategies.

APPENDIX A

SAMPLE POLICY ON INFORMATION ASSET PROTECTION

The following sample policy on information asset protection can be tailored to any organization and promulgated on paper and on the company intranet. It is adapted from the policy in the ASIS International *Information Asset Protection Guideline* (2007).

A. POLICY OVERVIEW

We are committed to protecting the organization's assets, including employees, information, and work environment, to enable us to achieve our business goals. As such, we have established this information asset protection (IAP) policy. It sets forth our guiding principles with respect to protecting the organization's information assets.

Information is a key organizational asset and will be protected commensurate with its value and based on the results of periodic risk assessments. The protection strategy is based on the following principles:

- Protecting information assets will consist of identifying, valuating, classifying, and labeling in an effort to guard against unauthorized access, use, disclosure, modification, destruction, or denial.

- Controls will represent cost-effective, risk-based measures consistent with other policies and the strategic goals of the organization.

- The IAP strategy integrates traditional security, information technology security, and legal and administrative functions.

- Responsibility and accountability extends to all employees as well as consultants, contractors, subcontractors, part-time employees, temporary employees, interns, teaming partners, and associates.

- We will meet all applicable legal and regulatory requirements.

B. IAP PROGRAM MANAGER

All questions, issues, and concerns related to this policy will be directed to the IAP program manager [*provide contact information.*]

C. APPLICABILITY

The IAP policy applies to all employees and to the extended enterprise—that is, individuals and entities with access to the organization's information assets, people, and facilities.

D. INFORMATION ASSETS

Our information assets fall into a variety of categories, some of which are subject to specific laws and regulations. In those cases, we will comply with all applicable laws and regulations. This may become complicated in some circumstances when laws and regulations at the local, state, federal, and international levels may all apply. Contact the organization's counsel or IAP program manager for guidance in specific cases.

The major categories of information assets include privacy information, proprietary information, trade secrets, patents, copyrights, trademarks, financial data, and regulated information. Each category warrants certain protections according to the IAP policy.

E. INFORMATION CLASSIFICATION AND SHARING

It is essential to share information both internally and externally to achieve our business objectives. However, it is also our responsibility to ensure that sensitive information assets are protected from loss or compromise. All employees and members of our extended enterprise are responsible for sharing information assets appropriately and protecting them from inappropriate disclosure, modification, misuse, or loss.

To protect information (paper, electronic, oral, etc.) according to its business value, we have developed policies, practices, and procedures as part of our IAP program. Included is a mechanism to classify our information assets into four categories: highly restricted, restricted, internal use, and unrestricted:

- *Highly restricted* is used for proprietary information that could allow a competitor to take action that could seriously damage our competitive position or that, if disclosed, could significantly damage the organization's financial or competitive position. Strict precautions are used to eliminate accidental or deliberate disclosure and to detect unauthorized attempted access. Access for employees is limited to specifically authorized individuals. Access for non-employees is limited to individuals who are approved and are covered by a nondisclosure agreement (NDA).

- *Restricted* is used for information that is organizationally or competitively sensitive or that could introduce legal or employee privacy risks. Precautions are taken to reduce accidental or deliberate disclosure. Access for employees is based on the individual's role. Access for non-employees is limited to individuals who are approved and are covered by an NDA.

- *Internal use* is used for information generated within the organization that is not intended for public distribution. Commonsense precautions are used to reasonably protect this information. Access is generally limited to employees. Access for non-employees is limited to individuals or organizations that are approved and are covered by an NDA.

- *Unrestricted* is used for information that can be shared inside and outside the organization.

Everyone is required to take these steps:

- Follow all procedures and practices regarding the protection of information assets.

- Participate in incident management, risk assessments, work processes, and control mechanisms that support the policy.

- Ensure that proper access controls are in place for any information you create or own.

- Use common sense and forethought in the release of organization-related information.

Employees in designated roles have been assigned specific responsibilities for the deployment, implementation, and maintenance of the IAP policy. These roles and responsibilities are as follows:

- The *IAP program manager* is responsible for overall policy, including

  - determining the levels and the protection required within each level

  - providing baseline information security through the organization's technology infrastructure

  - providing IAP management reports as appropriate

  - coordinating the program with other members of the organization

- *Other managers and directors* are responsible for employees' understanding of and compliance with the IAP policy as well as organizational practices and procedures. These managers and director may be responsible for

  - training employees on all classification levels

  - ensuring that work processes and controls support the policy

  - ensuring that risk assessments are conducted as needed and that incidents are managed within the framework of the IAP policy

F.   EMPLOYEE PRIVACY

Employee data is a resource to be protected against alteration, loss, or unauthorized disclosure. We guard information that is essential to running the business and protect this information from disclosure to anyone other than those who have a legitimate business need or legal right to have it.

The privacy and confidentiality of personnel records must be assured. Any personal information collected by the organization will be necessary and relevant and will be obtained and maintained using methods that respect the individual's right to privacy as well as applicable laws and regulations. In addition, each employee has the right to know what type of personal information the organization maintains about him or her and how it is or may be used.

Periodic audits may be conducted to ensure compliance with organizational policy as well as laws and regulations regarding privacy and personal information management.

G.   SECURING OUR PROPERTY

We are committed to providing security for our tangible and intangible assets to avoid loss. Each of us should do the following:

- Help ensure that access to the organization's facilities is limited to authorized persons or approved visitors.

- Wear and display appropriate identification as defined by organizational policy.

- Address security issues in a proactive manner, seeking early involvement of the security department in new brand initiatives, construction projects, and related issues.

- Be aware of and take appropriate action on potential security risks at work.

Managers in company branches will ensure that facilities meet recommended access control standards and comply with other security guidance and will respond to security incidents or concerns, ensuring they are properly reported to the security department.

The security department, in conjunction with other departments, has the responsibility to conduct any investigative activities in cases of known or suspected information loss, compromise, theft, manipulation, denial of access, fraud, or conflict of interest. Security also has the responsibility for involving local authorities as appropriate. Specialized expertise should be engaged through trusted external providers when appropriate.

Specific measures for handling, marking, storage, transmission and transport, copying, declassification, and destruction of sensitive information are provided in our organization's practices and procedures, available on our intranet.

H. SECURITY AWARENESS AND TRAINING

Each employee and member of the extended enterprise is responsible for protecting our information assets. Each individual must also be aware of the reasons or need for controls, as well as the practices and procedures that comprise our IAP program. Security, in conjunction with the IAP program manager, will provide periodic security awareness training that will include up-to-date information on the risks to information assets and prudent defensive measures. Awareness will also be facilitated through regular newsletter articles, reminders, and Web-based resources.

Our intention is to keep security at the forefront of peoples' minds and to give everyone the necessary IAP tools, such as easy and quick access to company practices and procedures and useful answers to any questions.

I. PUBLIC RELEASE OF INFORMATION

Direct all media inquiries to the external affairs director to ensure that public information is presented consistently and that information requests are monitored.

J. PUBLICATIONS AND PRESENTATIONS

We encourage the appropriate sharing of information through presentations and publications. Such sharing fosters innovation, networking, market development, public relations, and community awareness.

Any information shared must follow the IAP policy regarding security precautions for each respective classification level. Contact your manager if you have questions regarding the information to be shared.

The external affairs department should be informed of all planned presentations and publications to outside audiences. Presentations and publications that could potentially involve restricted or highly restricted information should be consistent with the organization's IAP policy.

K. TRAVEL SECURITY PLANNING

Information assets are particularly vulnerable when our employees and associates travel. Therefore, IAP-focused travel security training should be developed. The training should discuss the security environment of the travel destination and review relevant security practices and procedures. These may include visit requests or notifications, reporting procedures, material packaging or forwarding, and preparation of storage media. Any security issue, suspicious activity, or other problem encountered during the trip should be reported to the security department, the IAP program manager, or the traveler's own manager.

Notebook computers and handheld devices are particularly vulnerable to theft during travel. The use of wireless devices and networks outside of the organization's facilities is subject to restrictions outlined in the organization's practices and procedures. In addition, employees should not discuss sensitive information in public places where conversations can be over-heard or recorded—or with individuals who do not have a need to know.

L. NEW PROJECTS AND INITIATIVES

All new research, development, product line, or brand initiatives should be protected using the security principles and strategies detailed in the IAP policy and the supporting practices and procedures. An IAP plan should be considered for any projects involving highly restricted or restricted information.

M. IT RESOURCES

Computers, peripherals, and handheld and wireless devices owned or issued by the organization remain the property of the organization and are intended for business use only. All such systems and the information contained on them are subject to monitoring or review by the organization's officials or representatives, and no expectation of privacy exists in the possession or use of these systems.

Individuals (employees and members of the extended enterprise) are responsible for proper handling and protection of all hardware, firmware, software, data, and information associated with these systems. This includes ensuring that software is properly licensed and that the equipment is reasonably protected from theft, tampering, and misuse.

In addition, individuals are responsible for protecting all information that may reside on such systems, regardless of its sensitivity or subject matter. Information must be properly protected while resident on the system and while being processed, copied, transmitted, received, or exchanged.

Although a limited and reasonable amount of non-business use may be tolerated in some cases (e.g., receiving a personal phone call on a company mobile telephone), such use should be minimal and proper security measures still apply. Under no circumstances will any inappropriate matter (e.g., pornography, illegal activities, defamatory material, threats, etc.) be accessed, downloaded, stored, transmitted, or processed on company-owned or -issued systems.

N. WEB PRESENCE

Individuals must ensure that any information they post on-line follows IAP policy procedures for highly restricted, restricted, and internal use information.

O. TRUSTED RELATIONSHIPS (EXTENDED ENTERPRISE)

Specific obligations, practices, and procedures for IAP will be documented in written agreements prior to the execution of any contract, consulting engagement, or other business relationship that may involve the exchange of or access to sensitive information. The agreements may include an NDA, contract clauses, memoranda of understanding, or other formats. The agreement should specify the type of information to which it applies, the identity of the parties involved, the purpose of the agreement, and the time period for which it will remain valid. Specific reference to the IAP policy and other relevant organizational policies, practices, and procedures will be made in all such agreements.

Individuals and entities in a trusted relationship with our organization should be made aware that their obligation to protect certain information may extend beyond the period of their relationship with us or the end of a particular project. In addition to our written agreement, local, state, federal, or international laws and regulations may also apply to information protection and disclosure matters.

P. REPORTING SUSPICIOUS ACTIVITY OR SUSPECTED LOSSES OR COMPROMISES

Individuals should notify the IAP program manager or security department about (1) any inappropriate approaches (in person or electronic) by individuals requesting sensitive information, (2) any other suspicious activity, and (3) any suspected loss or compromise of sensitive information. These issues can be reported as follows [*list contact information*].

This organization abides by copyright, trademark, trade secret, and patent law.

Employees who violate this policy—either intentionally or through negligence—may be subject to disciplinary action, including possible termination. In addition, employees, individuals, and entities covered under this policy may be subject to administrative actions, criminal prosecution, or civil actions for violations.

APPENDIX B

QUICK REFERENCE GUIDE FOR INFORMATION ASSET PROTECTION

This guide is designed to help every employee or trusted associate of an organization determine the proper classification of material and relevant procedures for handling sensitive information. It is adapted from the ASIS International *Information Asset Protection Guideline*, May 2007.

STEP 1   This document is a quick reference guide for information asset owners and users. For more detailed information on specific topics, please see the policy, practices, and procedures manual available at _____.

Listed below are the four categories used to classify information and a brief explanation of the procedures to be followed for each classification. All information should be classified under one of the following four categories: Unrestricted, Internal Use, Restricted, or Highly Restricted. Only information under the categories of Internal Use, Restricted, or Highly Restricted is required to be marked. Share or disseminate this information following the procedures listed below for each category. If the information has not yet been classified, proceed to Step 2.

UNRESTRICTED	INTERNAL USE	RESTRICTED	HIGHLY RESTRICTED
This information can be shared within the organization and outside of the organization.	1. Read access is unrestricted within the company. Version control and updates are managed by the content owner. 2. Sharing externally without a nondisclosure agreement (NDA) requires a clear understanding between the parties that the information is to be treated as confidential. 3. This information is not to be shared with the public.	1. Content owners manage access lists and authorize sharing. 2. Access is limited to certain organizations, groups, or people in certain roles (i.e., legal, engineering, marketing, etc.) 3. Breadth and type of information access (e.g. create, read-only, update or delete) is limited and is based on role and fraud control requirements. 4. A signed NDA and an established "need to know" policy are required to share this information with the Extended Enterprise.*	1. Content owners manage access lists for type of access and authorized sharing. 2. Access is restricted to specifically named individuals with an established "need to know." 3. Authorizing a fellow employee requires verification of employee status and a clear understanding of intended use. 4. In authorizing sharing information with an individual from the Extended Enterprise, verify that a signed NDA and an appropriate contractual agreement are in place. 5. Quarterly review of continued access.

*   "Extended Enterprise" consists of both individuals and entities with access to the organization's information assets, people, and facilities.

STEP 2 Did you create or otherwise own the information?

NO, but I would like to share it. Share information following the guidance provided in the chart in STEP 1. If you have a strong feeling that unmarked information should be marked because it may have a value to competitors or may have proprietary value, contact the information owner to share your concerns. It is the information owner's or creator's responsibility to initially mark and update information classifications.

YES, I need to determine classification and I have the authority to classify my information. I will determine the information classification using the following questions. The column with the most selections suggests the protection classification. Caveats: (1) Use good business judgment when sharing any business information; and (2) Share documents in read-only form.

	UNRESTRICTED	INTERNAL USE	RESTRICTED	HIGHLY RESTRICTED
1. What competitive advantage does this information provide?	None	Possible advantage	Definite advantage	Significant advantage
2. Likelihood that a competitor is seeking this information?	None	Some likelihood	Likelihood exists	Strong likelihood
3. If this information was disclosed, lost, or changed:				
• Potential damage to organization's operations?	None	Some damage	Moderate damage	Severe damage
• Potential damage to an individual?	None	Some damage	Moderate damage	Severe damage
• Potential damage to organization's reputation or image?	None	Some damage	Moderate damage	Severe damage
• Loss of customer, shareholder, or business partner confidence?	None	Some chance	Good chance	Definite chance
• Loss of trade secret or patent protection?	None	Some chance	Good chance	Definite chance
• Loss of ability to be first to market?	None	Some chance	Good chance	Definite chance
• Loss of market share?	None	Some chance	Good chance	Definite chance
• Effect on the company's stock value or venture capital support?	None	Little effect	Moderate and short-term effect	Severe and long-term effect

Examples:

UNRESTRICTED	INTERNAL USE	RESTRICTED	HIGHLY RESTRICTED
• Factual information contained in organization's advertising and on its Web sites.	• Organization charts • Employee directories • Maps of the facilities	• Pre-patent data • Safety data • Product initiative reports • Customer data • Consumer insights • Personnel information • Sourcing plans	• Developmental formulas • Patent data • Consolidated financials • Stock actions • Global financial system information • Flagship brand strategy

If the information does not meet the minimum criteria for "Internal Use" above, it might be considered public information, unless it falls under a special category such as data restricted by financial, healthcare, or privacy regulations. Check with your IAP Program Manager.

PROTECTION REQUIREMENTS FOR SHARING INFORMATION WITHIN VARIOUS CLASSIFICATIONS

Listed below are examples and suggested procedures to follow for the marking and dissemination of documents. Note: International, federal, state, or local laws or regulations may supersede protection requirements. For all electronic systems, the employee must use the organization's owned or approved software, media, and tools.

	INTERNAL USE	RESTRICTED	HIGHLY RESTRICTED
Marking Documents (Paper and Electronic)	Only items with broad corporate circulation are marked "Internal Use" and these are shared in non-editable form.	Mark "Restricted" on the *first* page or mark at Application/Web site entry.	Mark "Highly Restricted" on *every* page and every screen that displays or provides access to Highly Restricted data.
Mailing/Shipping within the company	Routing envelope with no special markings.	Double, sealed envelopes. Mark inner envelope "Restricted: to be opened by addressee only." No security marks on outer envelope.	Double, sealed envelopes. Mark inner envelope "Highly Restricted: to be opened by addressee only." No security marks on outer envelope.
Facsimile (FAX) within the company	No special requirements.	Confirm fax number and ask if machine is physically secured. Ask recipient to be present while fax is received.	Avoid faxing across international borders, if possible. If sent, neutralize or sanitize contents to degree practical.
Facsimile (FAX) over outside lines	Notify recipient and confirm the fax number.	Ask recipient to be present while fax is received.	Fax if other more secure methods of transference are unavailable. 1. Neutralize/sanitize contents to degree practical. 2. Request recipient to be present during receipt. 3. Do not draw attention to sensitivity by marking cover sheet.
E-mail/Electronic Transfer within the company (Intranet, encrypted links, dedicated lines)	No special requirements.	Encryption is recommended but not required for internal electronic communications.	1. Encrypt e-mail messages or files, if possible. 2. Use encryption technology, if possible. 3. Validate business need and identity of the receiver.
E-mail/Electronic Transfer through outside networks (Internet)	1. Address to specific individuals. 2. Do not post on bulletin boards or send to public forums.	1. Use encryption technology, if possible. 2. Validate business need and identity of the receiver.	
Storage within the company	Use password enabled screensaver with timeout less than 15 minutes	1. Encrypt electronic documents and control access. 2. Maintain personal control or use locked storage.	
Storage off company premises	1. Keep information under your control. 2. Use password enabled screensaver with timeout less than 15 minutes.		
Destruction/Disposal	1. Where appropriate, adhere to the organization's retention limits. 2. Shred hard copy or use locked recycle bins. 3. Delete electronic information. 4. Destroy removable media (e.g., diskettes, CD's, tape cartridges, zip disks, etc.) before disposal.		

APPENDIX C

This appendix contains two sample nondisclosure agreements. The first protects the information assets of one party only, while the second provides mutual protection. For additional information, see Daniel B. Hassett, "Is Your Model Non-Disclosure Agreement Adequate?" *Wireless Watch*, April 2003, available at www.wileyrein.com/publication_newsletters.cfm?id =12&publication_ID=10040.

SAMPLE 1: NONDISCLOSURE AGREEMENT GOVERNING ONE PARTY'S INFORMATION

(Source: World Intellectual Property Association, September 2003, available at http://www.wipo.int/export/sites/www/sme/en/documents/doc/model_nda.doc)

THIS AGREEMENT is dated _____, 20[   ], and made

BETWEEN

(1)   [Name and address] .... ("Owner") and

(2)   [Name and address] .... ("Recipient")

WHEREAS

(A) Owner possesses certain Proprietary Information which Owner is willing to disclose to Recipient on the terms set out below

(B) Recipient is willing to accept the Proprietary Information on those terms and to use the Proprietary Information only for the purpose of .... ("the Permitted Purpose").

NOW IT IS AGREED AS FOLLOWS

1.   "Confidential Information" means any and all information whether commercial or technical relating to the business of Owner, including without limitation, know-how, data, processes, designs, photographs, drawings, specifications, software programs, and samples, which is marked with an indicator such as "Confidential" or "Proprietary", but excluding information which:

   1.1   is or comes into the public domain otherwise than by disclosure or default by the Recipient;

   1.2   was or is lawfully obtained or available from a third party who was lawfully in possession of the same and free to disclose it; or

   1.3   was already known to the Recipient as evidenced by written record pre-dating such disclosure.

2. In consideration of Owner disclosing Proprietary Information, the Recipient hereby under-takes for a period of [five] years from the date of this Agreement

    2.1   to keep confidential all Proprietary Information that it may acquire in any manner;

    2.2   to use such Proprietary Information exclusively for the Permitted Purpose and not to use the Proprietary Information for the Recipient's own purposes or benefit;

    2.3   not to disclose such Proprietary Information to anybody, except to authorized employees or other agents of the Recipient who need to have access to the Proprietary Information for the purpose of carrying out their duties in connection with the Permitted Purpose;

    2.4   to inform everybody to whom it discloses Proprietary Information that it is confidential and obtain their agreement to keep it confidential on the same terms as this Agreement;

    2.5   to keep safe any drawings, documents, samples or materials provided on loan by Owner, not to reproduce, part with possession of, modify or otherwise interfere with such items, to return them immediately upon Owner's request and in any event spontaneously when no longer required for the purposes of this Agreement;

    2.6   to notify Owner immediately upon becoming aware of any breach of confidence by anybody to whom the Recipient has disclosed the Information and give all necessary assistance in connection with any steps which Owner may wish to take to prevent, stop or obtain compensation for such breach or threatened breach.

3. Nothing in this Agreement shall be deemed to grant to the Recipient a license expressly or by implication under any patent, copyright or other intellectual property right. The Recipient hereby acknowledges and confirms that all existing and future intellectual property rights relating to the Proprietary Information are the exclusive property of Owner. The Recipient will not apply for or obtain any intellectual property protection in respect of the Proprietary Information. All intellectual property rights relating to any drawings, documents and work carried out by the Recipient (whether past, present or future) using the Proprietary Information will belong to and will vest in Owner. The Recipient will do all such things and execute all documents necessary to enable Owner to obtain, defend or enforce its rights in such drawings, documents and work.

4. This Agreement is governed by and will be construed in accordance with English law and is subject to the non-exclusive jurisdiction of the English Courts.

For and on behalf of Recipient: For and on behalf of Owner:

Signed: _____   Signed: _____

Name: _____   Name: _____

Position: _____   Position: _____

SAMPLE 2: NONDISCLOSURE AGREEMENT GOVERNING BOTH PARTIES' INFORMATION

Source: Gene Quinn, "Mutual Non-Disclosure Agreement," January 2008, available at http://www.ipwatchdog.com/tradesecret/mutual-confidentiality-agreement/

It is understood and agreed to that the parties to this Agreement would each like to provide the other with certain information that may be considered confidential. To ensure the protection of such information and in consideration of the agreement to exchange said information, the parties agree as follows:

1. The confidential information to be disclosed under this Agreement ("Confidential Information") can be described as and includes:

    Technical and business information relating to proprietary ideas, patentable ideas and/or trade secrets, existing and/or contemplated products and services, research and development, production, costs, profit and margin information, finances and financial projections, customers, clients, marketing, and current or future business plans and models, regardless of whether such information is designated as "Confidential Information" at the time of its disclosure.

    In addition to the above, Confidential Information shall also include, and the parties shall have a duty to protect, other confidential and/or sensitive information which is (a) disclosed as such in writing and marked as confidential (or with other similar designation) at the time of disclosure; and/or (b) disclosed by in any other manner and identified as confidential at the time of disclosure and is also summarized and designated as confidential in a written memorandum delivered within thirty (30) days of the disclosure.

2. The parties shall use the Confidential Information only for the purpose of evaluating potential business, employment and/or investment relationships.

3. The parties shall limit disclosure of Confidential Information within its own organization to its directors, officers, partners, members and/or employees having a need to know and shall not disclose Confidential Information to any third party (whether an individual, corporation, or other entity) without prior written consent. The parties shall satisfy its obligations under this paragraph if it takes affirmative measures to ensure compliance with these confidentiality obligations by its employees, agents, consultants and others who are permitted access to or use of the Confidential Information.

4. This Agreement imposes no obligation upon the parties with respect to any Confidential Information (a) that was possessed before receipt; (b) is or becomes a matter of public knowledge through no fault of receiving party; (c) is rightfully received from a third party not owing a duty of confidentiality; (d) is disclosed without a duty of

confidentiality to a third party by, or with the authorization of the disclosing party; or (e) is independently developed.

5. The parties warrant that they have the right to make the disclosures under this Agreement.

6. This Agreement shall not be construed as creating, conveying, transferring, granting or conferring upon either party any rights, license or authority in or to the information exchanged, except the limited right to use Confidential Information specified in paragraph 2. Furthermore and specifically, no license or conveyance of any intellectual property rights is granted or implied by this Agreement.

7. Neither party has an obligation under this Agreement to purchase any service, goods, or intangibles from the other party. Furthermore, both parties acknowledge and agree that the exchange of information under this Agreement shall not commit or bind either party to any present or future contractual relationship (except as specifically stated herein), nor shall the exchange of information be construed as an inducement to act or not to act in any given manner.

8. Neither party shall be liable to the other in any manner whatsoever for any decisions, obligations, costs or expenses incurred, changes in business practices, plans, organization, products, services, or otherwise, based on either party's decision to use or rely on any information exchanged under this Agreement.

9. If there is a breach or threatened breach of any provision of this Agreement, it is agreed and understood that the non-breaching party shall have no adequate remedy in money or other damages and accordingly shall be entitled to injunctive relief; provided however, no specification in this Agreement of any particular remedy shall be construed as a waiver or prohibition of any other remedies in the event of a breach or threatened breach of this Agreement.

10. This Agreement states the entire agreement between the parties concerning the disclosure of Confidential Information and supersedes any prior agreements, understandings, or representations with respect thereto. Any addition or modification to this Agreement must be made in writing and signed by authorized representatives of both parties. This Agreement is made under and shall be construed according to the laws of the State of _____, U.S.A. In the event that this agreement, is breached, any and all disputes must be settled in a court of competent jurisdiction in the State of _____, U.S.A.

11. If any of the provisions of this Agreement are found to be unenforceable, the remainder shall be enforced as fully as possible and the unenforceable provision(s) shall be deemed modified to the limited extent required to permit enforcement of the Agreement as a whole.

WHEREFORE, the parties acknowledge that they have read and understand this Agreement and voluntarily accept the duties and obligations set forth herein.

Recipient of Confidential Information:

Name (Print or Type): _____

Company:_____

Title: _____

Address: _____

City, State, Zip: _____

Signature: _____

Date: _____

Disclose of Confidential Information:

Name (Print or Type): _____

Company: _____

Title: _____

Address: _____

City, State, Zip: _____

Signature:_____

Date: _____

APPENDIX D

TECHNICAL REPORTS AND LABORATORY NOTEBOOKS

MANAGING TECHNICAL REPORTS

Enterprises with research and development facilities must pay particular attention to technical reports and laboratory notebooks as part of their information asset protection (IAP) strategy. First, it makes good business sense, and second, proper procedures for handling these documents will ensure a strong legal base in the event of a trade secret or patent infringement suit.

Policy makers sometimes fail to consider the interdependent steps leading to the production of a technical report. This may cause a situation where there is an elaborate system for the protection of the finished product but relatively little concern for the many intermediate steps. *However, it is in the intermediate stages that the greatest possibility of compromise with the least prospect of detection often occurs.* This, in part, is why an intensive and thorough audit and reporting system is required.

As indicated in the chart, the most vulnerable period for the potential loss of critical information is in the intermediate phases of a project. Generally, information available early in a project, particularly a research effort, is related to basic science and is often not considered to be highly sensitive. Protection measures are not very robust at this point, so they usually match the sensitivity of the information fairly well.

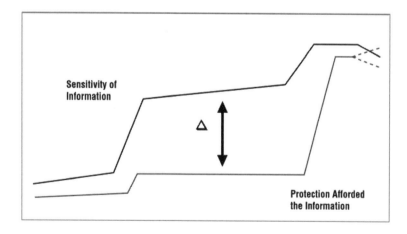

During market research and near product rollout, there may be a fair amount of sensitive Information, but there are usually robust safeguards in place—again a good match between levels of sensitivity and protection.

In the middle phases, however, the sensitivity and amount of information related to the initiative generally grows rapidly, sometimes in an unanticipated manner. Information protection measures may not be a high priority or may not catch up with the amount or sensitivity of the information. Similarly, key personnel may not realize the significance or sensitivity of the information at this point. Finally, this period is usually longer than other project phases, and players may become complacent about information protection. For these reasons, this is generally the period of time when the information is most vulnerable to both intentional and inadvertent threats (Peterson, 2005).

Another issue often overlooked is how information is stored and handled once the product has been marketed or the technical report published. Often, attention has shifted to a new product under development, and material is transferred to a different storage location, which may be under the control of employees unfamiliar with the importance of the data. This is a perfect example of why an effective IAP program must incorporate cradle-to-grave protection, including control of secondary distribution of technical reports and access to the raw data. This is in addition to the protection of the end product or process, which is generally more straightforward.

The consequences of a loss may be time-dependent. In other words, the compromise of a particular trade secret or bit of proprietary information may have enormous impact on a project at the applications research phase, but only a minor impact at the marketing phase. Timing, time dependencies, and project phases should always considered when measuring the potential consequences of a loss of information.

Timeline of a Technology-Based Commercial Product
(Peterson, 2005)

The timelines involved in a research or development project can be lengthy, adding to the complexity of the IAP approach. Initial research, development efforts, raw data, testing results, prototype items, intermediate production test runs, and technical data must all be considered assets to be protected as well as any finished products, reports, and processes.

PROCEDURES FOR LABORATORY NOTEBOOKS

The following are general guidelines for managing and protecting laboratory notebooks.

1. GENERAL

Keeping laboratory notebooks is part of the professional responsibility of scientists and engineers. Well-documented laboratory notebooks are an important asset to the company since, for example, they help avoid repetitive experimental work, permit retracing of steps to isolate critical aspects of a new discovery or invention, establish legally significant documentation of an invention or discovery, and permit proper determination of inventor status.

The requirement to maintain legally adequate documents for patent purposes is the most stringent. Therefore, notebooks properly maintained for that purpose will normally be adequate for all other purposes. The requirements for patent records have been established through legal precedents in which courts consider an inventor's testimony as inadequate to establish proof of his own invention. In all cases, the courts require that the inventor's testimony be buttressed by that of disinterested parties having firsthand knowledge of the making of the invention.

2. BASIC LEGAL PRINCIPLES

The procedures for managing laboratory notebooks are based on several basic legal principles, summarized as follows:

2.1 A completed invention is comprised of two events:

- Conception of the idea

- Reduction to practice (demonstrating the usefulness of the data for the intended purpose)

2.2 The inventor's testimony and records alone are not sufficient to establish conception and reduction to practice. The testimony must be substantiated in every respect by others.

2.3 Conception, being wholly within the inventor's mind, can be proved only by his or her disclosure to others.

2.4 Conception is best proven by a written document disclosing the invention in complete form, dated, signed by the inventor, and witnessed by someone else who understands the invention.

2.5 Reduction to practice (actual carrying out of the invention) must be proven (corroborated) by someone else who can swear that he or she either

- watched the inventor carry out all the important aspects of the invention or

- personally carried out the invention on behalf or at the direction of the inventor.

2.6 Neither the witness of conception nor the corroborator of reduction to practice may be a co-inventor. Where two or more joint inventors are involved, no one of them can corroborate any other joint inventor. The testimony of any one of them must be corroborated by someone else who is not one of the joint inventors.

2.7 Both the witness of conception and the corroborator of reduction to practice must understand the invention.

2.8 The testimony of the witness and of the corroborator should be supported by tangible evidence prepared at the time. Such evidence may be in the form of writings, sketches, drawings, blueprints, samples, models, etc.

2.9 Undated or predated documents are not admissible evidence.

3. MINIMUM LEGAL REQUIREMENTS IN MAINTAINING NOTEBOOKS FOR PROVING CONCEPTION AND REDUCTION TO PRACTICE

In the light of the previous rules, the following practice must be followed by each employee engaged in laboratory work involving research and development:

3.1 On the conception of an original idea, the inventor must immediately document this idea in a notebook with appropriate sketches, drawings, and discussion in order that one knowledgeable in the field involved can understand it. The notebook entry must then be dated and signed by the inventor. The notebook entry must then be read and understood by two witnesses who sign at the bottom as follows:

"Witnessed, read, and understood by _____(name) on _____(date)."

3.2 Reduction to practice by the inventor can be proven only by the testimony of someone else who personally observed the reduction to practice and knew what was done. The reduction to practice may be performed by the inventor or by another at the inventor's direction. In the case of a process invention, the corroborator of reduction to practice need observe only the essential steps of the process. The reduction to practice must likewise be documented in a laboratory notebook. But blueprints, drawings, purchase orders, etc., concerning the reduction to practice may be incorporated by reference into the notebook by making clear and positive identification of these documents. The entry concerning reduction to practice should be made by the inventor or the party making reduction to practice on behalf of the inventor in his or her own notebook and then signed and dated by the inventor. The entry must then be read and agreed to by two persons who witnessed, firsthand, the essential aspects of the reduction to practice.

These corroborating witnesses cannot be co-inventors, but should be persons knowledgeable in the scientific field involved who are working on other projects. After reading the entry and agreeing thereto, the corroborating witnesses must sign directly below the entry as follows:

"Witnessed, read, and understood by _____(name) on _____(date)."

If a reduction to practice takes place over a long period of time, each significant step must be entered into the notebook on the date made and witnessed in the manner described above.

3.3 The following administrative details must be observed in using and managing laboratory notebooks:

3.3.1 The notebook must be bound and not loose leaf.

3.3.2 Each entry should, in general, set forth why the work was done, what was done, who did it when, with what results, and the conclusions drawn from the results.

3.3.3 All entries in the notebook must run consecutively without blank spaces. All unused portions must be blocked out, dated, and signed.

3.3.4 Coded terminology must not be used unless the code is fully defined in the notebook. Commonly accepted abbreviations are permissible.

3.3.5 The record must not be falsified.

3.3.6 The record must not be altered. Any errors that occur must not be erased or altered. Instead a single line should be drawn through the error and the corrections made immediately thereafter. Earlier entries may be corrected or revised by a new entry which makes specific reference to the earlier one.

3.3.7 All entries must be made with ink or indelible pencil.

3.3.8 Entries must not be backdated.

3.3.9 All records must be kept current since any delay in recording matters of conception or reduction to practice seriously diminishes the value of the entry. The entry made must be sufficiently complete so that one skilled in the art can understand the invention. Any critical ranges or optimum points must be specifically set forth.

3.3.10 Any efforts which fail or do not work as expected should likewise be entered. But caution should be exercised to avoid sweeping, negative conclusions.

4. NOTEBOOK CONTROL

4.1 Each new employee engaged in laboratory work involving research and development must acquire a notebook from the research librarian.

4.2 All notebooks will be numbered consecutively by the research librarian and will be registered in the librarian's name and issued directly to the individual who will use the notebook.

4.3 A completely filled notebook must be returned to the research librarian, but the notebook may be kept at the office of the author for reference purposes.

4.4 On termination, an employee will return all notebooks to the research librarian. Any other employee who is to continue the work may have the registration of notebooks transferred in order that they may be kept in his or her office for reference purposes.

5. DISCLOSURE OF INVENTIONS

5.1 After making notebook entries as set forth above, an invention disclosure should be completed as set forth in Standard Procedure.

5.2 Employees will not disclose notebook data and information concerning inventions to anyone outside the company except in compliance with standard release procedures.

6. PROVISIONS FOR ELECTRONIC LABORATORY NOTEBOOKS

6.1 In today's environment organizations are increasingly using electronic laboratory notebooks either in lieu of or in addition to hard copy notebooks.

6.2 Where electronic laboratory notebooks are in use, they will be protected in a manner commensurate with the procedures outlined above and consistent with the organization's policies on IAP and IT security.

6.3 Controls should be in place to prohibit or carefully manage the removal of electronic laboratory notebooks from the facility where they are normally used and stored. With the prevalence of theft of electronic devices and the ability to easily transfer, alter, or copy enormous amounts of data, the integrity of laboratory notebooks is highly vulnerable to compromise.

APPENDIX E

INFORMATION DISPOSAL AND DESTRUCTION

The following is based on material from the National Association for Information Destruction (www.naidonline.org) and is used by permission.

Every business has information that requires destruction.

Customer lists, price lists, sales statistics, drafts of bids and correspondence, and even memos contain information about business activity that would interest any competitor. Every business is also entrusted with information that must be kept private.

Without the proper safeguards, information ends up in the dumpster, where it is readily and legally available to anybody. Any establishment that simply discards private and proprietary data exposes itself to the risk of criminal and civil prosecution and business losses.

Stored records should be destroyed on a regular schedule.

No record should be kept longer than is necessary for business or compliance purposes. By routinely destroying stored records, a company can avoid appearing suspicious in the event of litigation or an audit. Regular destruction also limits the amount of material a company must provide in legal proceedings.

Incidental business records discarded daily should be protected.

The daily trash of every business contains information that could be used against it. Such records include phone messages, memos, and drafts of bids and correspondence.

Recycling is not an adequate alternative for information destruction.

Recycling does not equal secure destruction. Paper is given away or sold, and there is no practical means of establishing whether and when a document was destroyed. It is better to arrange for recycling after materials are properly destroyed.

Due diligence is essential.

Any company contracting an information destruction service should require that it provide a signed testimonial documenting the date that the materials were destroyed. The certificate of destruction, is an important legal record. It does not, however, transfer responsibility for the confidentiality of the materials to the contractor.

If private information surfaces after the contractor accepts it, a court may question the process by which the contractor was selected. Any company not showing due diligence in their selection of a contractor could be found negligent. Due diligence could consist of a review of the contractor's policies and procedures and initial and follow-up site audits.

Most records storage companies do not provide secure shredding services themselves.

If the storage company subcontracts its destruction services, the client must conduct a due diligence investigation of the document destruction company used.

REFERENCES

ASIS International. (2007). *Information asset protection guideline*. Alexandria. VA. Available: http://www.asisonline.org/guidelines/guidelinesinfoassetsfinal.pdf [2008, August 14].

ASIS International. (2007). *Trends in proprietary information loss*. Alexandria, VA. Available: http://www.asisonline.org/foundation/noframe/loss.pdf [2008, August 14].

ASIS International Information Asset Protection Council. (2005). *IAP toolkit*. Available: http://www.asisonline.org/councils/InfoToolkit.exe [2008, August 14].

Crowdy, T. (2006). *The enemy within: A history of espionage*. Westminster, MD: Osprey Publishing.

Federal Bureau of Investigation. Focus on economic espionage. Available: www.fbi.gov/about-us/investigate/counterintelligence/economic-espionage [2011, April 6].

Hassett, D. B. (2003, April). Is your model non-disclosure agreement adequate?, *Wireless Watch*. Available: www.wileyrein.com/publication_newsletters.cfm?id=12&publication_ID=10040 [2008, August 14].

Kramer, L. A., Heuer, R. J., Jr., & Crawford, K. S. (2005). *Technological, social and economic trends that are increasing U.S. vulnerability to insider espionage*. PERSEREC Technical Report 05-10. Monterey, CA: Defense Personnel Security Research Center.

Microsoft Corporation. (2006). *Regulatory Compliance Planning Guide*. Available: http://www.microsoft.com/technet/security/guidance/complianceandpolicies/compliance/rcguide/default.mspx?mfr=true [2008, August 14].

Moberly, M. D. (2006). Positioning intellectual property, intangible assets and proprietary competitive advantages to beat the odds against counterfeiting and piracy. White paper. Memphis, TN: Knowledge Protection Strategies.

Moberly, M. D. (2007). Risk assessments and due diligence for business transactions. White paper. Memphis, TN: Knowledge Protection Strategies.

Peterson, K., CPP. (2005). A strategic approach to information protection for small businesses and organizations: Getting started. White paper. Herndon, VA: Innovative Protection Solutions.

Poteat, S. E. (2001, Winter). The attack on America's intellectual property: Espionage after the Cold War, *The Bent of Tau Beta Pi*.

Sun Tzu. (1983). *The art of war*. Ed. J. Clavell. New York, NY: Dell Publishing.

United States Department of Energy. Espionage and the Manhattan Project (1940-1945). Available: www.mbe.doe.gov/me70/Manhattan/espionage.htm [2008, August 14].

United States Department of Justice. (2006). *Progress report of the Department of Justice's task force on intellectual property.* Available: http://www.usdoj.gov/opa/documents/ipreport61-906.pdf [2008, August 14].

United States General Accountability Office. (2007, April 12). Intellectual property: National enforcement strategy needs stronger leadership and more accountability. Statement of Loren Yager, Director International Affairs and Trade.

United States Office of the National Counterintelligence Executive. (2006). *Annual report to Congress on foreign economic collection and industrial espionage—2005.* Available: http://www.fas.org/irp/ops/ci/docs/2005.pdf [2008, August 14].

United States Patent and Trademark Office. Inventor resources. Available: http://www.uspto.gov/web/offices/com/iip/index.htm [2008, August 14].

United States Secret Service and Carnegie Mellon Software Engineering Institute. (2005). *Insider threat study: Computer system sabotage in critical infrastructure sectors.* Available: http://www.cert.org/archive/pdf/insidercross051105.pdf [2008, August 14].

Winkler, I. (2005). *Spies among us.* Hoboken, NJ: Wiley Publishing.

World Intellectual Property Organization. (2003). Non-disclosure agreement. Available: www.wipo.int/sme/en/documents/disclosing_inf.htm [2008, August 14].

CHAPTER 2
THE INCREASING IMPORTANCE OF INFORMATION SYSTEMS SECURITY

In the movie *Ocean's Eleven*, casino owner Terry Benedict discovers that Danny Ocean has compromised the state-of-the-art video monitoring system protecting Benedict's vault and its millions in cash. The attack against the supposedly uncrackable security system relied in part on hacking into information systems. The film depicts Benedict as one who takes the protection of his money very seriously, and he gives his security personnel no second chances. In the real world, too, cybercriminals take advantage of security weaknesses in corporate information systems every day, stealing, destroying, misappropriating, or otherwise misusing corporate assets.

Cybercrime—the use of information systems to commit crime—is real. In May 2009, President Obama said, "It's been estimated that last year alone cyber criminals stole intellectual property from businesses worldwide worth up to $1 trillion" (Obama, 2009). Information systems are beset with vulnerabilities unlike those in the physical world. To address the never-before-seen challenges of information system security (ISS), security professionals must augment their physical security paradigm with a new logical security paradigm (Lam & Stahl, 2010).

In *The Structure of Scientific Revolutions* (1962), Thomas Kuhn revolutionized the way philosophers think about science. He introduced the word *paradigm* as a theoretical tool for understanding all the things one thinks about when one considers a scientific school of thought or other rigorous discipline, like physical security or ISS. From this perspective, the physical security paradigm is the framework used in processing issues specifically focused on the realms of physical security, such as cameras, perpetrators, protection of human life, and securing facilities against physical losses. The framework comprising the logical security paradigm deals with similar issues, but the losses occur in the virtual space, where they are invisible from a physical perspective and thus require a different understanding to counter them.

The purpose of this part of the *Protection of Assets* is to provide the security professional already knowledgeable in the physical security paradigm with a practical understanding of a new logical security paradigm.

2.1 **THE HUMAN CHALLENGE: FAILURE OF IMAGINATION**

On September 11, 2001, terrorists flew planes into the twin towers of the World Trade Center and into the Pentagon. A fourth plane crashed in Pennsylvania, instead of its intended target, only as a result of the heroic efforts of passengers. The FBI and other U.S. intelligence agencies had all the dots they needed to see 9/11 coming. Had they connected the dots, over 3,000 people might have been saved. Why were the dots not connected? In the final report from the 911 Commission (National Commission on Terrorist Attacks, 2004, p. 336), one answer given was a "failure of imagination."

Here's another, far less serious example of a failure of imagination. At the door of a hotel pool, guests would insert their key cards into a slot, open the door, and enter the pool area. Security seemed to be working perfectly—that is, until a young girl walked up to the door, stuck her thin hand through the bars below the latch, reached up, and opened the door.

At a Web site log-in screen, users might be expected to enter their user ID and password, much as swimming pool guests might be expected to enter their card keys in the door's slot. However, a user might be able to access the site by entering *'' or 1=1 –"* or even something very complicated like the following:[2]

> http://www.sanitized.net/Communications/PhoneList/directory.asp?fieldValue0=1'%20UNION%20ALL%
> 20select%20'',name,'','','','','','%20from%20MASTER..SYSDATABASES&fieldName0=EE_ID&fieldType
> 0=202&fieldValue1=&fieldName1=LastName&fieldType1=202&fieldValue2=&fieldName2=FirstName&field
> Type2=2202&fieldValue3=CLO&fieldName3=Off_ID&fieldType3=202&fieldValue4=&fieldName4=DeptID&f
> ieldType4=202&fieldValue5=&fieldName5=DiscID&fieldType5=2&fieldValue6=&fieldName6=Extension&fie
> ldType6=202&fieldValue7=&fieldName7=DirecDial&fieldType7=202&fieldValue8=&fieldName8=Cell&fieldT
> ype8=202&fieldValue9=&fieldName9=Pager&fieldType9=202&fieldValue10=&fieldName10=Month&fieldTy
> pe10=5&fieldValue11=&fieldName11=Day&fieldType11=5&fieldValue12=&fieldName12=eeJobTitle&fieldT
> ype12=202&fieldValue13=&fieldName13=exeTitle&fieldType13=202&fieldsCount=14&sqlSelect=LastNam
> e%2CFirstName%2CExtension%2CDirecDial%2CCell%2CPager%2CeeJobTitle%2CexeTitle&sqlWhere
> =&act=dbSheetView&db=sanitizednet&dbTable=Employees&passwd=&order1=LastName&a=b&order2=
> FirstName&order3=&LastName1=LastName&FirstName1=FirstName&Extension1=Extension&DirecDial1=
> DirecDial&Cell1=Cell&Pager1=Pager&eeJobTitle1=eeJobTitle&exeTitle1=exeTitle

Attacks like these—with arcane names like *SQL-injection, cross-site scripting, content spoofing,* and *information leakage*—are like the thin wrists on the young girl who entered the swimming pool without a key, often providing the cybercriminal access to back-end corporate assets.[3]

---

[2] This second example is sanitized code used in a penetration test to obtain Social Security numbers and other sensitive information from a supposedly secure database.

[3] Cross-site scripting carried out on Web sites accounted for more than 80 percent of documented security vulnerabilities in the second half of 2007 (Symantec, 2008, pp. 1-3).

Before this type of attack occurred, no one had imagined it. Even after it was imagined, many Web sites continue to be vulnerable to such attacks, giving hackers full access to the underlying information.

Not long ago, a corporate information technology (IT) director wrote the following about his employer's susceptibility to on-line bank fraud:

> Teresa has a fob that issues pass codes, which change every 30 seconds. The fob is not connected to the computer in any way. To complete an authorized transaction on the computer she needs to enter a pass code from the fob within that 30 second time frame. **I can't imagine a way that a hacker would be able to manage** [**to hack**] **that.** [Emphasis added.]

Yet two weeks earlier, a *Washington Post* article about the theft of $447,000 from a company's bank account had this to say about the security of multi-factor authentication, like Teresa's fob (Krebs, 2009):

> Some types of malware, particularly a type of data-stealing Trojan horse programs known as "Zeus," allow the attackers to change the display of a bank's login page as a victim is entering their credentials. For example, when a victim submits his one-time password along with his credentials, the malware may force the browser to return a counterfeit page (still showing the bank's domain name in the URL bar) stating that the bank's site is down for maintenance, please try back again in 15 minutes. Meanwhile, those credentials are not submitted to the bank but instead sent to the attackers.

> This tactic is remarkably effective: When an unwitting customer waits as instructed, the thieves use those intercepted credentials to log in as the victim and initiate unauthorized transfers from that account.

Failures of imagination are part of being human. After experiencing a bad situation, a person can imagine similar scenarios. The challenge lies in situations a person has not experienced before.

2.2 STATE OF INFORMATION SYSTEMS SECURITY

The microcomputer revolution—and with it the rise of local-area networks, wide-area networks, and the Internet—was 35 years old in 2010.[4] Interconnecting computers and networks has brought great gains in productivity and opened up exciting new realms of entertainment and information. It has brought the world closer together. However, these virtues are not without unintended, and sometimes undesired, consequences.

On July 1, 2003, California Senate Bill 1386—the nation's first breach-disclosure law—became effective. The law requires any organization conducting business in California to notify affected residents should the organization have reason to believe that unencrypted personal information of California residents has been acquired by an unauthorized person.[5] Most states have now followed California with their own breach-disclosure laws, and a national law is likely.

In the slightly more than six years since California's law went into effect, the Privacy Rights Clearinghouse (2009) has identified more than 340 million consumer records as having been breached.

Here are just a few of the many companies that have acknowledged suffering data breaches:

Choicepoint	T.J.Maxx	Ernst & Young	JP Morgan
Sam's Club	Citi Financial	Ralph Lauren	DSW
MCI	Kodak	Motorola	Deloitte
Bank of America	Time Warner	Ford Motor	Hanover

The figure of 340 million includes only reported breaches. It does not include discovered but unreported breaches, undiscovered breaches, or other data losses—such as thefts from on-line banking—that do not legally need to be disclosed.

The 340 million breached data records represent only the tip of the iceberg. They also illustrate how cybercrime has changed over the last few years. In the past, the greatest information systems threats were internal. Few hackers existed; of those who did, most were in it for their egos, and most of the damage they caused was limited to theft of computer resources and the denial of service resulting from virus attacks.

---

[4] Malcolm Gladwell dates the start of the microcomputer revolution as January 1975, when "the magazine *Popular Electronics* ran a cover story on an extraordinary machine called the Altair 8800" (Gladwell, 2008, p. 63).

[5] California Civil Codes 1798.29, 1798.82, and 1798.84.

The hackers who used to hack for pleasure or to increase their reputation are now in it for money (Herley & Florencio, 2009). They are becoming more sophisticated and learning to circumvent defenses. One source reports that "the bad guys are adapting to our current protection strategies and inventing new ways to attain the data they value" (Verizon Business RISK Team, 2009, p. 47).

In July 2009, cybercriminals were targeting YouTube account holders with phishing attacks (Harwood, June 2009). On August 17, 2009, three men were indicted for stealing more than 130 million credit card numbers. They were able to get in by scanning for vulnerabilities in corporate Web sites (Trotta, 2009). Also in August of 2009, the social network site Twitter was disabled as hackers attempted to retaliate against a single user but brought down the entire site (Acohido, 2009). Incidentally, it took almost 100,000 bots (software applications that run automated tasks) under the control of the hackers to bring the site down. It cost about $5,000 to rent those bots. In addition, new ways to access wireless networks to the detriment of business continue to be found (Mills, 2009).

In congressional testimony, a computer security expert observed the following about hacker attacks (Kellerman, 2009):

> cyber-attacks have become a wholly pervasive phenomenon based in part on:
>
> - Increasing connectivity and availability of assailable network, systems and applications vulnerabilities.
>
> - The ability of cybercriminals to derive significant financial rewards through successful attacks.
>
> - Worldwide federation between various classes of cybercriminals and malware developers.
>
> - Nation-state, terrorist and politically driven backing of targeted cybercrime efforts.
>
> - A lack of cohesive law enforcement around the globe.

Cyber extortion has begun to rear its ugly head and is now a problem for corporate America (Wagley, 2009). Cybercriminals have figured out that they do not need to change their malware as quickly but can implement it on more sites (Harwood, August 2009). In addition, they use automated techniques that continually compromise legitimate Web sites, increasing the chance users will eventually get redirected to an illegitimate site. Moreover, criminals are changing malware code so it is not detected by traditional antivirus systems.

Perhaps the most serious challenge is the recent rash of on-line bank thefts. According to the FBI (2009), cyber thieves hacking into small- and medium-sized organizations have stolen about $100 million out of U.S. bank accounts. Some of these attacks are sophisticated enough to defeat two-factor authentication systems.

A Computer Security Institute (CSI) Computer Crime and Security Survey (Richardson, 2008) found that the average financial cyber fraud cost the victim company $500,000, and an average bot attack—an attack by compromised computers, sometimes numbering in the hundreds of thousands—cost $350,000. Such attacks can have serious impacts. One case affected the operations of a Seattle hospital (U.S. Attorney's Office, 2006). The CSI report also notes that 27 percent of attacks in 2008 were targeted attacks where a piece of malware was written directly to attack a specific company.

Verizon's investigation of 500 breaches found that over the course of these breaches, 285 million records were stolen (Verizon Business RISK Team, 2009). The study found that 74 percent of the records were stolen by external sources. Kellerman (2009) corroborates the view that insiders are no longer the cause of most losses.

Additionally, the CSI report notes that minor hacks continue to be a problem. Mischele Kwon, former director of the United States Computer Emergency Readiness Team (US-CERT) calls such hacks a "hygiene problem" (Kwon, 2009), that is, a known problem that can be fixed with due diligence. However, it is the more sophisticated attacks that are obtaining most of the stolen records (Verizon Business RISK Team, 2009).

The Verizon report observes that the professionalism of computer crime is growing. The threat is no longer from "script kiddies" but from organized crime consortiums, which have the funds to conduct more-sophisticated attacks. In fact, Verizon found that 91 percent of records stolen in 2008 were taken by organized crime groups. CSI notes that firewalls and antivirus programs are "fundamentally imperfect," and that malware and other attacks can circumvent signature-based controls. In addition, Verizon states that in the more successful breaches, someone was able to take advantage of an error committed by the victim and installed malware to take advantage of it.

The news is not all bad. Apparently, there is a glut on the underworld market for credit card numbers, so now personal identification numbers (PINs) are the hot items (Verizon Business RISK Team, 2009, p. 7):

> The potential value of engaging in cybercrime would not exist without a market for stolen data. As with any legitimate market system, the unit value of goods and services fluctuates with supply and demand. ... Criminals have reengineered their processes and developed new tools—such as memory-scraping malware—to steal this valuable commodity. This has led to the successful execution of complex attack strategies previously thought to be only theoretically possible.

Moreover, custom malware is on the rise. Verizon estimates that 8 percent of the 285 million records breached were taken with custom malware created specifically for the attack.

Criminals are also hiding their work, creating challenges for those who have to catch them or investigate the aftermath of the crimes. Investigators found "anti-forensics"—attempts to hide one's tracks—in over one-third of the cases in Verizon's research.

Also growing is the use of cyberspace by governmental entities. For example, in 2008, "the nation-state of Georgia was attacked by hackers, presumably from Russia" (Willson, August 2009). Wilson also writes about attacks against Estonia and the use of cyber warfare in clashes between Israel and Hamas. In July 2009, South Korean Web sites were also allegedly attacked by North Korea (Kim, 2009).

Rogueware, or software that pretends to be security software but really compromises a computer, is also on the rise. Cybercriminals are estimated to be making $34 million a month by getting users to download this malicious software (Correll, 2009).

Now, even phones are not safe. Mobile malware is an up-and-coming profit center for criminals (Dunham, 2009). Users' phones could be compromised before they even begin conducting phone-based banking.

Stewart Baker, former U.S. assistant secretary of homeland security, offers this summary (2009):

> In fifteen years, decentralized networks have moved from novelty uses like monitoring communal coffee machines to managing financial assets, telecommunications, and the electric grid. That's both good news and bad, because this revolutionary new technology poses real risks. We trust far more of our critical assets to IT networks than we once did, and security vulnerabilities that may have been tolerable fifteen years ago can have devastating consequences today.

An IBM report concludes that "every Web site should be viewed as suspicious and every user is at risk" (IBM Global Technology Services, 2009).

The crimes and the situations described in this section affect systems that security professionals use in their day-to-day work and that they are charged with protecting. Security professionals must educate themselves in the ways of information security—and also stay abreast of ongoing changes.

2.3 ECONOMICS OF INFORMATION SYSTEMS SECURITY

Information security incidents cost money. For example, of a computer virus is the loss in productivity of an organization's personnel plus the time and expense for IT personnel to remove the virus and restore availability. Often the loss of productivity is more costly than the cost of cleaning up from the virus attack. In one case, removing a virus from a law firm's network required three days of work by two IT staff and two consultants, costing the firm approximately $2,400 in staff time and another $10,000 in consultant fees. Meanwhile, the firm estimated that the productivity of its 100 attorneys fell by 20 percent. The cost in lost billings exceeded $25,000, more than double the cost of cleaning up the virus attack.

The cost of a theft of a trade secret by a cyber thief is the value of the trade secret to the company. Companies must ask themselves what it would cost them if a competitor had intellectual property like their customer lists, pricing information, cost structure, strategic plans, or proprietary processes.

The cost of the theft of customer social security numbers includes the cost of notifying customers plus any identity theft services provided to protect customers plus legal expenses if lawsuits are filed plus the loss of good will. The average cost to comply with state breach-disclosure laws now exceeds $200 per record (Claborn, 2009). This translates to breach-disclosure costs of more than $2 million for a breach of a relatively tiny 10,000 person database.

Implementing security also has costs. Firewalls and other ISS technologies take capital away from other uses. Should a company invest in a new sales management system or augment its current signature-based antivirus system with a more modern behavior-based host intrusion prevention system?

Information systems security (ISS) personnel come at the expense of personnel who can more directly contribute to the bottom line. A new salesperson might contribute $1 million or more in new sales. What does an information security analyst contribute to the bottom line?

Every hour management spends in a security meeting, or personnel spend on security awareness training, is an hour that could otherwise also contribute to the bottom line.

In basic risk management, how much one should spend to prevent an ISS incident equals the probability of the incident times its cost (Gordon & Loeb, 2006). Related to risk management is a company's legal duty to take steps to secure its information assets. This point was made more than 60 years ago by Judge Learned Hand in *United States v. Carroll Towing Co.* (1947), in which Hand wrote that a party is negligent if the cost (B) of taking adequate measures to prevent harm is less than the monetary loss (L) multiplied by the probability (P) of its occurring (B < PL).

As ISS incidents grow in number and the cost of recovery climbs, companies must be prepared to invest more of their resources in prevention. Using corporate resources effectively to protect sensitive information and systems is one of the key objectives of an ISS program (Braun & Stahl, 2005). Such a program consists of all the activities and expenditures the organization takes to protect sensitive information. The program may be formal, with a specific executive tasked with management responsibility (recommended), or informal, with activities and expenditures done as needed. Either way, the program's objective should be to prudently and cost-effectively manage the risk that critical information could

- be compromised,

- be changed without authorization, or

- become unavailable.

2.4 CRITICAL SUCCESS FACTORS

Three coevolving domains define whether a company's ISS program meets an information security standard of due care:

- legislation and regulation regarding the duty of information holders to protect nonpublic information about others in their computer systems

- contract and tort law on the securing of information and information assets

- recommended security practices of the professional ISS community

In *An Emerging Information Security Minimum Standard of Due Care* (2005), Braun and Stahl analyze those three domains and identify seven critical success factors that an information security standard of care must meet:

- **Executive management responsibility.** Someone at the top has management responsibility for the company's information security program, which is managed in accordance with its information security policies.

- **Information security policies.** The company has documented its management approach to information security in a way that complies with its responsibilities and duties to protect information.

- **User awareness training and education.** Users receive regular training and education in information security policies and their personal responsibilities for protecting information.

- **Computer and network security.** IT staff is securely managing the technology infrastructure in a defined and documented manner that adheres to effective ISS practices.

- **Third-party information security assurance.** The company shares information with third parties only when it is assured that those parties protect the information with at least the same standard of care as does the company.

- **Physical and personnel security**. The company provides appropriate physical protection for information, screens candidates for employment, and incorporates information security in job responsibilities.

- **Periodic risk assessment.** The company conducts an assessment or review of their ISS program, preferably by an independent party, covering both technology and management, at least annually.

An eighth factor—classifying and controlling sensitive information—is typically part of information security policy framework recommendations (as in ISO 27001 and 27002). This factor calls for a company to understand the laws, regulations, and contracts that impose information security obligations on it; identify its intellectual property that requires protection; inventory sensitive information and implement appropriate security measures to protect it; distinguish information as public, for internal use, or restricted; and assign information owners to be responsible for defining who needs access to what information. Non-ISS staff gain a better understanding of ISS when this eighth factor is included.

2.5 IMPLICATIONS TO PHYSICAL SECURITY IN A CONVERGED WORLD

The convergence of physical and information security has numerous definitions. The Alliance for Enterprise Security Risk Management provides this basic definition (Booz Allen Hamilton, 2005, p. 3):

> the identification of security risks and interdependencies between business functions and processes within the enterprise and the development of managed business process solutions to address those risks and interdependencies.

Here is a more detailed definition (Tyson, 2007, p. 4):

> Security convergence is the integration, in a formal, collaborative, and strategic manner, of the cumulative security resources of the organization in order to deliver enterprise-wide benefits through enhanced risk mitigation, increased operational effectiveness and efficiency, and cost savings.

Convergence allows physical security devices to interact across a network for substantial organizational gains. At the same time, it creates significant additional risk to the organization because the physical security devices are now accessible from anywhere on the network. In the old paradigm, video cameras, video recorders, intrusion detection systems, and bank accounts were not accessible unless a person physically approached them. Now they are potentially accessible from anywhere in the world.

A good summary of these issues comes from congressional testimony by the director of Sandia National Laboratories' Information Operations Center (Varnado, 2005):

> Today, the legacy systems are gradually being replaced by new SCADA [supervisory control and data acquisition] systems that use the Internet as the control backbone. This change is being implemented to reduce cost and increase efficiency of operation. However, this trend substantially increases the possibility of disruptions because (1) the number of people having access to the system is substantially increased, (2) disruptions can be caused by hackers who have no training in control systems engineering, and (3) the use of the Internet exposes SCADA systems to all the inherent vulnerabilities of interconnected computer networks that are currently being exploited by hackers, organized crime, terrorists organizations, and nation states. Worms, viruses, network flooding, no-notice attacks through compromised routers, spyware, insider attacks, data exfiltration by outsiders who gain insider privileges (phishing), and distributed denial of service attacks are all commonplace. Effectively combating these attacks requires increased awareness, new technology, and improved response and recovery capabilities.

This paradigm is virtually identical to the current situation in the physical security realm.

Figure 2-1 shows a traditional video surveillance system, in which one would need physical access to the system to compromise it. Physical access to the system could be prevented with a fence, a security officer, or other measures.

Figure 2-1
Video-to-Recorder Layout

Figure 2-2 shows a modern video surveillance layout.

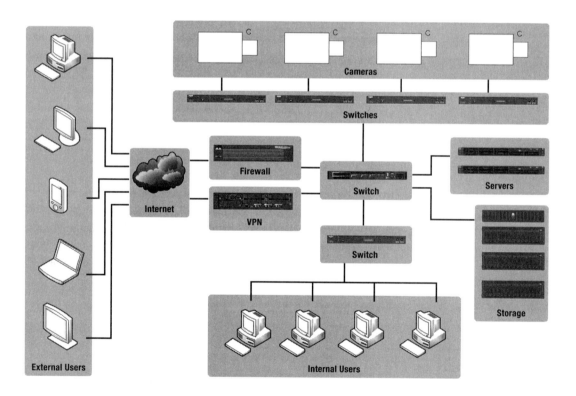

Figure 2-2
Video Infrastructure

Multiple computers on the network are able to access a server that now stores video data. Cameras on the network are putting that video data on that same server.

Physical security can use several modes of communication. First, there may be a proprietary connection between one device and another. Second, there may be an industry-standard connection between two devices, such as the Weigand protocol between a card reader and controller. Third, network devices generally speak over TCP/IP (transmission control protocol/Internet protocol), the worldwide Internet standard for communication.

Devices may be divided into two types of systems, embedded and host-based. Embedded systems (also known as special systems) are typically programmed at the manufacturer and run proprietary or nonstandard operating systems. These may include video cameras, card readers, access controllers, intrusion detection (alarm) control panels, analog-to-digital video converters, and so on. Host-based systems run on more standard operating systems, typically a Windows or Linux operating system (the Macintosh OS runs on a flavor of UNIX, sister to the Linux operating system). Embedded systems are far more difficult to change than Windows operating systems, but all these systems can be compromised.

Since any system that communicates with something else is potentially compromiseable, physical security practitioners need to make informed decisions on what systems can go where. For example, Underwriters Laboratories (UL) has strict rules on how fire systems must be implemented, especially given the life-safety issues that arise from those systems. What if a physical security intrusion detection system server was taken over and rendered useless by persons bent on accessing the location?

IP video surveillance provides many advantages over earlier systems, but it too is vulnerable. Security professionals should ask themselves these questions:

- What if someone took over a camera?
- What if someone placed a video stream recorded earlier in place of the original stream?
- Does the equipment manufacturer put into place any controls to make this difficult or impossible?
- What if terrorists were watching the video stream?
- What if thieves turned off the switch that brings video into the system?
- What if someone erased video evidence?
- What if someone turned off video analytics so no alarms were sent to the security officer?
- What if a burglar tuned the video analytics function so that it repeatedly caused false alarms?

Likewise, electronic access control provides many security benefits, yet it too is vulnerable. Access control systems typically contain three major components and up to two different transport media. The card reader is typically the part that the user sees, and presents a card to, either a contact mechanism or a contactless method, sometimes called a "prox" (proximity) card. The card reader communicates over some medium, either wired or wireless, to a controller that decides whether the door should open or something else should happen (although these two systems can be integrated). Finally, the controller typically talks to a server or an application from which it gets its instructions on what to do and what card information to store locally.

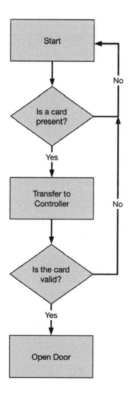

Figure 2-3
Basic Access Control Card Flow

Traditional access control systems have been compromised in a number of non-network ways. First, most access control cards do not require mutual authentication before giving up their secret number on the card. A legacy HID (Hughes identification device) card has two components: the secret facility number, which is not printed on the card but is known to the facility owner, and an identification number that is printed on the card. When a card reader requests this number, a combination of the secret and printed number, the card simply supplies it. If it were as easy to get someone's house key as it is to walk up within a foot of a person with a scanner in a backpack or purse and thereby get the card information, one would be quite worried. Yet many companies are still using or buying systems based on this modality.

The second large vulnerability that applies to access control systems that are not accessible from the Internet or any other network centers around a protocol called Wiegand. Many current access control systems are based upon this protocol, developed in the late 1980s, which uses a plain-text mechanism to pass the credentials between the reader and the control panel.

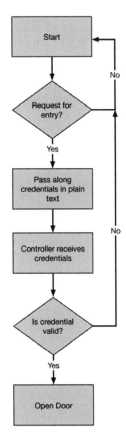

Figure 2-4
Basic Wiegand Flow

Unfortunately, since plain-text information is not scrambled, anyone who can gain access to the wire can gain access to the information. A tool called a gecko, which can be built for $10 worth of parts, can give an intruder complete control over a door. Clearly it is important to become educated on the possible risks associated with any device, even if the physical security elements are not converged with networks.

In typical networked access control implementations, access control systems run directly on the network. The network is generally made up of two parts: the embedded systems connection between a reader and a controller and then a TCP/IP network on which controllers talk to servers and users talk to servers.

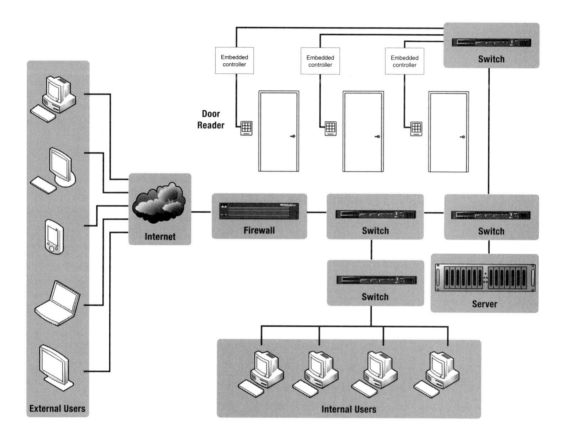

Figure 2-5
Networked Access Control System

Almost every access control system in use today runs a database on a computer. The database determines when someone can get in, what the rules are for that access, and whether a card is enabled or disabled. A person who can control the computer can make those changes.

Two dangers arise. First, a valid administrator could add a backdoor or additional card. Therefore, it is essential to employ information security risk assessment methodologies to be sure of appropriately applying rules to the system. Even authorized administrators should not be able to do the wrong thing easily, and if they do the wrong thing anyway, an audit trail should show what happened.

Second, the system may be accessible to the Internet. A server may be accessible only from certain other machines, but one of those machines could be taken over by a malicious individual. If that happened, a company's entire access control system could be in the hands of an unknown person.

Security professionals should use both intelligence and imagination to make good decisions when implementing their systems. No system is impervious to being changed, stopped, or modified externally if it is connected to a TCP/IP network or computer.

2.6 CYBERCRIME: A NATIONAL CHALLENGE

President Obama's speech on securing the nation's cyber infrastructure provides several useful observations. The following are excerpts from that speech; after each is a comment applying the President's remarks to the concerns of the security professional (Obama, 2009):

> It's the great irony of our Information Age—the very technologies that empower us to create and to build also empower those who would disrupt and destroy. And this paradox—seen and unseen—is something that we experience every day.

Technology enables security experts to do more than ever before in managing organizations' risk. However, it is also necessary to understand and apply a logical security paradigm to effectively protect assets.

> It's about the privacy and the economic security of American families. We rely on the Internet to pay our bills, to bank, to shop, to file our taxes. But we've had to learn a whole new vocabulary just to stay ahead of the cyber criminals who would do us harm—spyware and malware and spoofing and phishing and botnets. According to one survey, in the past two years alone cyber crime has cost Americans more than $8 billion.

Cybercrime is costing citizens and businesses a great deal of money. The stakes are high.

> This is a matter, as well, of America's economic competitiveness. The small business-woman in St. Louis, the bond trader in the New York Stock Exchange, the workers at a global shipping company in Memphis, the young entrepreneur in Silicon Valley—they all need the networks to make the next payroll, the next trade, the next delivery, the next great breakthrough. E-commerce alone last year accounted for some $132 billion in retail sales.

The problem affects not just one's own company but also the company's partners.

> But every day we see waves of cyber thieves trolling for sensitive information—the disgruntled employee on the inside, the lone hacker a thousand miles away, organized crime, the industrial spy and, increasingly, foreign intelligence services. In one brazen act last year, thieves used stolen credit card information to steal millions of dollars from 130 ATM machines in 49 cities around the world—and they did it in just 30 minutes. A single employee of an American company was convicted of stealing intellectual property reportedly worth $400 million. It's been estimated that last year alone cyber criminals stole intellectual property from businesses worldwide worth up to $1 trillion.

The threat comes from multiple threat vectors, which security professionals are in a position to stop.

In short, America's economic prosperity in the 21st century will depend on cybersecurity.

The success or failure of each organization may depend on security professionals' actions.

Our technological advantage is a key to America's military dominance. But our defense and military networks are under constant attack. Al Qaeda and other terrorist groups have spoken of their desire to unleash a cyber attack on our country—attacks that are harder to detect and harder to defend against. Indeed, in today's world, acts of terror could come not only from a few extremists in suicide vests but from a few key strokes on the computer—a weapon of mass disruption …

For all these reasons, it's now clear this cyber threat is one of the most serious economic and national security challenges we face as a nation.

In 1937, Alan Turing created the Turing Machine, the predecessor to what would ultimately become the microcomputer. His machine created a new world, a new paradigm which those responsible for protecting people and assets must now understand. The threat is real and the attacks are already well under way.

REFERENCES

Acohido, B. (2009, August 9). Twitter troubles show fragility of social network. *USA Today*.

Baker, S. (2009, April 28).*Testimony before the U.S. Senate Committee on Homeland Security and Governmental Affairs.* Available: http://hsgac.senate.gov/public/index.cfm?FuseAction=Files. View&FileStore_id=98c47739-98ac-43d5-a161-0fa82e2f5243 [2010, December 5].

Booz Allen Hamilton. (2005). *Convergence of enterprise security organizations.* Arlington, VA: Alliance for Enterprise Security Risk Management.

Braun, R., & Stahl, S. (2005). An emerging information security minimum standard of due care. In H. Tipton and M. Krause (Eds.), *Information security management handbook* (6th ed.). Boca Raton, FL: Auerbach Publications.

Claborn, T. (2009, February 3). Data loss costing companies $6.6 million per breach. *Information Week*.

Correll, S. (2009, September). Rogueware on an explosive trend. *ISSA Journal*.

Dunham, K. (2009, August). Mobile malcode threats. *ISSA Journal*.

FBI. (2009, November 3). Press release: Fraudulent automated clearing house (ACH) transfers connected to malware and work-at-home scams. Available: http://www.fbi.gov/pressrel/press rel09/ach_110309.htm [2010, December 5].

Gladwell, M. (2008). *Outliers: The story of success*. New York, NY: Little, Brown and Company.

Gordon, L., & Loeb, M. (2006). *Managing cyber-security resources: A cost-benefit analysis*. New York, NY: McGraw-Hill.

Harwood, M. (2009, August). Cybercriminals keep malware alive longer. *Security Management*.

Harwood, M. (2009, June). YouTube account holders target of phishing scam. *Security Management*.

Herley, C., & Florencio, D. (2009). Nobody sells gold for the price of silver: Dishonesty, uncertainty and the underground economy. Microsoft research. Available: http://research.microsoft.com/ pubs/80034/nobodysellsgoldforthe priceofsilver.pdf [2010, December 5].

IBM Global Technology Services. (2009). IBM Internet Security Systems X-Force 2009 mid-year trend and risk report. Available: http://www.servicemanagementcenter.com/main/pages/ IBMRBMS/SMRC/ShowCollateral.aspx?oid=68843&ssid=66&sf=1 [2010, December 5].

ISO 27001. (2005). *Information technology—security techniques—information security management systems—requirements.* Geneva, Switzerland: International Organization for Standardization.

Kellerman, T. (2009, April 28). Testimony before the United States Senate Homeland Security and Government Affairs Committee. Available: http://hsgac.senate.gov/public/index.cfm?FuseAction=Hearings.Hearing&Hearing_ID=fd18b89f-b540-4e9a-9c52-823013751b9b [2010, December 5].

Kim, H. (2009, July 9). Official says seven South Korean websites attacked again. *USA Today.*

Krebs, B. (2009, September 9). Cyber thieves steal $447,000 from wrecking firm. *Washington Post.* Available: http://voices.washingtonpost.com/securityfix/2009/09/cyber_theives_steal_447000_fro.html#more [2010, December 5].

Kuhn, T. (1962). *The structure of scientific revolutions.* Chicago, IL: University of Chicago Press.

Kwon, M. (2009, September 20). Speech to the ISSA gala 25 year anniversary event.

Lam, D., & Stahl, S. (2010, January). Convergence, paradigm shifts and reaching the village. *ISSA Journal.*

Lemos, R. (2009, September 18). Real-time hackers foil two-factor security. *Technology Review* (MIT). Available: http://www.technologyreview.com/computing/23488/?a=f.

Mills, E. (2009, August 24). Cisco wireless LANs at risk of attack, 'skyjacking.' *CNET News.* Available: http://news.cnet.com/8301-27080_3-10316870-245.html [2010, December 5].

National Commission on Terrorist Attacks. (2004). *The 9/11 commission report: Final report of the National Commission on Terrorist Attacks upon the United States.* New York: W.W. Norton.

Obama, B. (2009, May 29). Remarks by the President on securing our nation's cyber infrastructure. Available: http://www.whitehouse.gov/the-press-office/remarks-president-securing-our-nations-cyber-infrastructure [2010, December 4].

Privacy Rights Clearinghouse. (2009). Chronology of data breaches. Available: http://www.privacyrights.org/data-breach [2010, December 4].

Richardson, R. (2008). *CSI computer crime & security survey.* Available: http://www.cse.msstate.edu/~cse6243/readings/CSIsurvey2008.pdf [2010, December 5].

Symantec Corporation. (2008). *Symantec internet security threat report: Trends for July-December 2007.* Available: http://eval.symantec.com/mktginfo/enterprise/white_papers/b-whitepaper_exec_summary_internet_security_threat_report_xiii_04-2008.en-us.pdf [2010, December 5].

Trotta, D. (2009, August 17). Three indicted in largest US identity theft scheme. Reuters. Available: http://www.reuters.com/article/idUSTRE57G4GC20090817 [2010, December 5].

Tyson, D. (2007). *Security convergence: Managing enterprise security risk*. Burlington, MA: Butterworth-Heinemann.

United States v. Carroll Towing Co., 159 F.2d 169, 173-74 (2d Cir. 1947).

U.S. Attorney's Office, Western District of Washington. (2006, August 25). Press release: California man sentenced for "botnet" attack that impacted millions. Available: http://www.usdoj.gov/usao/waw/press/2006/aug/maxwell.html [2010, December 5].

Varnado, S. (2005, October 18). Statement to U.S. House of Representatives Committee on Homeland Security, Subcommittee on Economic Security, Infrastructure Protection, and Cyber Security and the Subcommittee on Emergency Preparedness, Science, and Technology. Available: http://www.sandia.gov/news/resources/testimony/pdf/051018.pdf

Verizon Business RISK Team. (2009). *2009 Data Breach Investigations Report*. Available: http://www.verizonbusiness.com/resources/security/reports/ 2009_databreach_rp.pdf.

Wagley, J. (2009, August). Preparing for cyber extortion. *Security Management*. Available: http://www.securitymanagement.com/article/preparing-cyber-extortion-005952 [2010, Dec-ember 5].

Willson, D. (2009, August). A global problem: Cyberspace threats demand an international approach. *ISSA Journal*.

CHAPTER 3
THE INFORMATION SYSTEMS SECURITY BODY OF KNOWLEDGE

The objective of an organization's information systems security (ISS) program is to prudently and cost-effectively manage the risk that critical organizational information could

- be compromised,

- be changed without authorization, or

- become unavailable.

In other words, the security professional strives to protect information's confidentiality, integrity, and availability (sometimes called CIA in this context). The effort is important because information systems risk leads to other business risks, such as the following:

- loss of money through theft, fraud, and embezzlement

- incident recovery costs

- costs for lost productivity

- loss of intellectual property

- attorney and other legal expenses

- loss of brand value

This part of the *Protection of Assets* presents an overview of the ISS body of knowledge, including ISS risk and numerous technical, legal, and management challenges.

3.1 **THE ELEMENTS OF ISS RISK**

3.1.1 **ISS TERMS**

The basic language of ISS may already be familiar to the traditional security practitioner:

- **Information systems threat:** any circumstance, capability, action, or event with the potential to adversely impact an information system through unauthorized access, destruction, disclosure, modification of data, and/or denial of service.[6]

- **Information systems vulnerability:** a flaw or weakness in an information system's design, implementation, or operation and management, including policies, procedures, processes, and internal controls that could be exploited to violate the system's security policy.[7]

- **Information systems risk:** product of level of threat and level of vulnerability.[8]

- **Information systems countermeasure:** an action, device, procedure, technique, or other measure that reduces a threat, a vulnerability, or an attack by eliminating or preventing it, by minimizing the harm it can cause, or by discovering and reporting it so that corrective action can be taken.[9]

---

[6] This definition combines the definitions of the Committee on National Security Systems Instruction (CNSSI) 4009, the SANS (SysAdmin, Audit, Network, Security) Institute, and RFC2828 (Internet Security Glossary). CNSSI 4009 defines "threat" as "any circumstance or event with the potential to adversely impact an information system through unauthorized access, destruction, disclosure, modification of data, and/or denial of service." SANS and RFC2828 define "threat" somewhat analogously as "potential for violation of security, which exists when there is a circumstance, capability, action, or event that could breach security and cause harm." The primary difference is that CNSSI 4009 is more explicit about the meaning of "breach security" and "cause harm."

[7] This definition of vulnerability is an amalgam of CNSSI 4009 and RFC2828. CNSSI 4009 defines "vulnerability" as any "weakness in an IS, system security procedures, internal controls, or implementation that could be exploited." RFC2828 define "vulnerability" as a "flaw or weakness in a system's design, implementation, or operation and management that could be exploited to violate the system's security policy."

[8] This definition is from the SANS Institute, well-known in the information systems security community for managing the Internet Storm Center and for the quality of its training programs. CNSSI 4009 defines "information systems security risk" as the "possibility that a particular threat will adversely impact an IS by exploiting a particular vulnerability." A common variation is to include the amount of loss in the definition of risk. For example, RFC2828 defines "information systems security risk" as the "expectation of loss expressed as the probability that a particular threat will exploit a particular vulnerability with a particular harmful result."

[9] CNSSI 4009 defines a "countermeasure" as an "action, device, procedure, technique, or other measure that reduces the vulnerability of an information system." RFC2828 defines it as "an action, device, procedure, or technique that reduces a threat, vulnerability, or attack by eliminating or preventing it, by minimizing the harm it can cause, or by discovering and reporting it so that corrective action can be taken."

- **Residual threat risk:** for each threat, the remaining potential risk after all ISS countermeasures are applied.[10]

- **Residual risk:** the total remaining potential risk after all ISS countermeasures are applied across all threats.[11]

3.1.2 FUNDAMENTAL EQUATION OF ISS

The risk concepts above connect together in the fundamental equation of ISS (Quigley & Stahl, 1987):

$$\text{Residual Risk} \; = \; \frac{\text{Threats} \; * \; \text{Vulnerabilities}}{\text{Countermeasures}}$$

This equation is intended to be qualitative, not quantitative. It says that residual risk rises as threats rise and as vulnerabilities rise. Residual risk falls as countermeasures are applied. All other things being equal, the more vulnerabilities one has, the higher one's residual risk is. Similarly, the more carefully planned and managed a system of countermeasures is, the lower the residual risk is.

3.1.3 INFORMATION SYSTEM THREATS

Threats are carried out by threat agents. The first two categories of threat agents are already familiar to physical security practitioners. The third category illustrates the need for a logical (as opposed to physical) security paradigm. The categories are:

Nature:

- earthquakes
- hurricanes
- other natural disasters

---

[10] This is simply called residual risk in the National Institute of Standards and Technology's Glossary of Key Information Security Terms, (NISTIR 7298, 2006).

[11] This definition integrates the NIST definition of residual risk with the ISO 27001:2005 definition of residual risk ("risk remaining after risk treatment") and RFC2828's "the risk that remains after countermeasures have been applied."

People:

- employees and others with legitimate access who desire to take advantage of opportunities

- cybercriminals and others without legitimate access

    - on-line bank thieves

    - botnet herders

    - thieves engaged in credit card fraud and identity theft

    - corporate spies

    - foreign governments engaged in cyber warfare

    - angry, hostile, or deranged individuals or groups engaged in cyber terrorism

Virtual Threat:

- a computer program or script illegitimately installed on a workstation, server, router or other information systems device and capable of any or all of the following:

    - sending information from the device on which it is installed to the owner of the program (its control)

    - receiving command and control instructions from its control and adjusting its behavior accordingly

    - executing commands on the device on which it is installed

A virtual threat agent is the equivalent of a ghost in the network, a ghost one may not even know is present until, acting on behalf of its real-world owner, it steals, changes, or destroys an organization's information or misuses its system.

Virtual threats do not exist in the real world. To rob an actual bank vault, one must go to the bank. A criminal cannot tell Scotty to "Beam me up" and expect to be transported into the vault and then back out with the loot. By contrast, the virtual equivalent of this is done every day in cyberspace. More than anything else, the cybercriminal's ability to "go virtual" is what makes the logical security paradigm so different from the physical security paradigm.

Virtual threats take advantage of the very logic of modern computer and communications systems. Such systems are so complex that their logic is inherently flawed. These flaws are the source of an unending stream of vulnerabilities. Cybercriminals and others take advantage of these vulnerabilities—often with the unwitting assistance of humans—to get their virtual threat agents installed and running on technology platforms.

Before using a virtual threat agent, a cybercriminal or other perpetrator must get it onto a target computer. Methods include direct physical access to the computer (via USB drive or other peripheral); hacking into the computer remotely; placing malware on the computer, perhaps while the user is visiting a Web site; and phishing and social engineering.

Some virtual threats current as of this writing include these:

- **marketing spyware,** collecting information about Web sites visited, sending the information to its owner, and displaying pop-ups

- **keyloggers,** recording keystrokes and sending the data to their owner

- **Koobface,** a computer worm that targets people who use social networking sites

- **Zeus**, an on-line banking Trojan

3.1.4 INFORMATION SYSTEM VULNERABILITIES

Threats cannot manifest without a vulnerability to exploit. ISS vulnerabilities fall into five broad categories

- **vulnerabilities in the information systems infrastructure**, such as inappropriate links to unprotected networks, improper system configuration, or unpatched workstations

- **vulnerabilities in people using the information systems infrastructure (users)**, meaning users allow other people, via social engineering or other means, to access their computers

- **vulnerabilities in people maintaining the information systems infrastructure (custodians)**, including too many permissions, inadequate monitoring and logging of actions, and inadequate training

- **executive and senior management vulnerabilities,** including lack of accountability, inadequate policies and procedures, inadequate security awareness training, inadequate third-party management, and physical vulnerabilities

- **vulnerabilities in information systems management processes,** including inadequate management control of information system infrastructure, inadequate patch management, inadequate change control, inadequate protection of networks and devices, inadequate software development and database administrator methodologies, and inadequate information continuity planning

3.1.5 **INFORMATION SYSTEM CONTROL OBJECTIVES**

Before outlining the range of countermeasures available for managing residual information system risk, it is important to specify the ISS control objectives that those countermeasures must meet.

Just as in other security disciplines, it is not enough to say one protects corporate assets. Three other control objectives must be met: detection, recovery, and compliance. As Figure 3-1 shows, for each of the four control objectives it is necessary to maintain the organization's data's confidentiality, integrity, and availability.

	Protect information systems	Detect system attacks, both successful and blocked	Recover from attacks	Comply with laws, regulations, contractual obligations
Confidentiality	✓	✓	✓	✓
Integrity	✓	✓	✓	✓
Availability	✓	✓	✓	✓

Figure 3-1
ISS Overall Objectives and Control Objectives

3.1.6 **INFORMATION SYSTEM COUNTERMEASURES**

As in other security disciplines, information systems countermeasures can be divided into three broad classifications:

administrative controls: management, policies, standards, procedures, guidelines, personnel screening, awareness training, etc.

technical controls: network log-ins and passwords, firewalls, audit logs, encryption, antivirus, and spam filters

physical controls: door locks, cameras, environmental controls, guards, etc.

In addition to classifying countermeasures by type, it is valuable to classify countermeasures by where they are implemented:

- countermeasures on the information systems infrastructure (technical)

- information systems infrastructure management countermeasures (administrative, technical, physical)

- executive and senior management countermeasures (administrative, technical, physical)

- community-based countermeasures (administrative, technical, physical)

Each of the preceding is addressed below.

Infrastructure Countermeasures

Infrastructure countermeasures are controls placed on the information system infrastructure to prevent the exploitation of threats. Such countermeasures include the following:

- **perimeter security,** including devices that create or secure a perimeter, such as switches, firewalls, etc.

- **device protection security,** including specific protection on devices (antivirus, desktop firewalls, encrypted hard drives, etc.)

- **access control and authentication,** including making sure a person is authorized before they can do anything on a device (user IDs, passwords, second-factor key fobs, etc.)

Information Systems Infrastructure Management Countermeasures

Countermeasures in this category include systemic rules for protecting the entire system. They include the following:

- **vulnerability and patch management**, to address any known vulnerabilities on one's system

- **system monitoring and log review**, to know what is happening on one's systems and be able to forensically investigate anything that occurs

- **information systems security metrics**, to ensure that one can measure the success of one's endeavors

- **physical security of the information systems infrastructure**, to make sure people cannot gain physical access to systems

- **IT staff training in information security**, to make sure that those to whom an organization entrusts its systems are properly trained

Executive and Senior Management Countermeasures

Perhaps most important in information security, as in physical security, is to have the buy-in of executive management in supporting security initiatives. Management countermeasures include the following:

- an explicit ISS management system with responsibility, authority, and accountability vested throughout the organization; leadership exercised from the top; and clear responsibilities for all managers and employees

- information security policies and procedures that incorporate ISS across the entire organization, including executive management

- ISS awareness training and education programs for all users

- incorporation of information system security matters in business continuity, contingency, and emergency plans

- information security management incorporated in all third-party information sharing agreements and implementations.

Community-Based Countermeasures

In a sense, it takes a village to secure a village. The widespread vulnerabilities across computer systems worldwide put everyone at increased cyber risk. Authors writing in the *ISS Journal* note (Lam, Pease, Stahl, & Takamine, 2007):

> In today's world, everyone is at risk from cyber crime. And, it will take us all to lower the risk to acceptable levels. Information Security no longer simply involves those working in the field as professionals. In today's world, everyone must participate in lowering the risk. Every IT manager, IT vendor, CIO, CTO, CFO, COO, CSO, and CEO; every member of every Board of Directors; every employee, whether in IT, purchasing, audit, sales, or HR must be a part of the Information Security solution. Every computer user has a role to play in lowering the community's information risk. We security professionals cannot secure our organizations by ourselves.

Everyone in business (including executives, frontline personnel, and security managers) and in community organizations is responsible for information security. A single machine left unpatched can be the launching pad for a series of attacks on everyone else.

3.2 DOWN THE RABBIT HOLE: COMPUTER LOGIC, SYSTEM COMPLEXITY, AND INHERENT VULNERABILITY

In 1936, a young British mathematician, Alan Turing, published a paper that can be considered the beginning of the modern computer age. In it he mathematically explored what it means for a number to be computable, i.e., for its successive decimal places to be calculable by finite means. The resulting mathematical framework that he created is now known as a Turing Machine, a machine for calculating the decimal places of numbers. Mathematically, every computer is nothing more than a finite Turing Machine, an incredibly sophisticated device for performing what are essentially very simple logical operations.

Every school child, for example, learns to compute the decimal places of simple fractions like ½, ¾, ⅔, ⅞, etc. Progressing through school, one learns algorithms for computing the decimals of square roots and the decimal expansion of numbers like Pi.

What Turing did in his monumental paper of 1936 was explicitly investigate the mathematical character of the seemingly simple concept of computability. In doing so, he discovered that the concept was anything but simple; in the 75 years since his paper, the theory of computability has become a rich and deep part of mathematics, lying at the heart of the logical foundations of mathematics.

Three years after publishing his paper and with the outbreak of World War II, Turing began applying his mathematics to the challenge of decrypting German signals. In doing so, he and his colleagues designed and built the world's first modern computer. Ironically, this first computer can be thought of as a hacker tool used to decrypt highly sensitive confidential German information!

Central to Turing's work—and to understanding the security challenges of modern computer systems—is the concept of an algorithm. An algorithm is a precise method for solving a problem using a finite sequence of precise instructions.

Computer programs are extremely large, extremely complex algorithms. Because of their size and their complexity, computer programs contain errors or bugs. These errors are sometimes the result of not being precise enough in defining the problem to be solved, the instructions to be followed, or the order in which the instructions are processed. These errors can result in information security vulnerabilities. To understand the logical security paradigm and what it means to information systems security, it is important to understand some of the challenges of writing good algorithms, i.e., software that contains relatively few (and relatively harmless) bugs.

3.2.1 **HOW COMPUTER SYSTEMS WORK**

The first digital computers built during World War II by Turing and others were designed to do one thing, to run one program. In the 70 years or so since then, computers have evolved in size, speed, and complexity. In 1968, when Intel was founded by Robert Noyce and Gordon Moore, no one really had any idea of what was to come. As Intel grew, Moore developed a hypothesis, now known as Moore's Law, that the processing power in any line of computers will double every 18 months. To some researchers on the border of anthropology and computer science, Moore's Law characterizes the exponential growth of human technologies going back more than 100,000 years.[12]

Why this is relevant to the physical security practitioner? The processing power in a BlackBerry smartphone or Apple iPhone is greater than that in the first PCs released by IBM in 1981. An implication of Turing's work is that more complexity, enabled by more processing power, leads to a greater possibility of error. Not only that, but these devices are interconnected in ways not even imaginable when Intel was founded.

As computers are used in new and innovative ways and become more interconnected, they become more vulnerable. Perfectly illustrating this are the physical security systems now running as part of converged technologies on IT networks around the world. What was previously understood as a physical asset now presents a new type of risk because it is a virtual asset. Because it is the realm of the physical security practitioner to protect these systems, whether they are cameras or alarms, and whether they exist physically, virtually, or both, it is now necessary for the physical security practitioner to understand how these devices interrelate and what additional risks they might pose to the organization.

As elsewhere in the virtual world, there is a small but vital subtlety here: a program can do what it is programmed to do and still contain vulnerabilities. The reason is that security is inadequately specified. For example, a security spec may say that the user interface to a back-end sensitive database requires a log-in ID and password. The database system is built in accordance with this spec but allows anyone with direct access to the back-end database to read the data. What the spec should have said is that no access to the data is permitted without the user being authenticated at the time of access. Now the back end can no longer assume that a user has already been authenticated at the front end.

---

[12] See, for example, Kurzweil (1999) and Wright (2000).

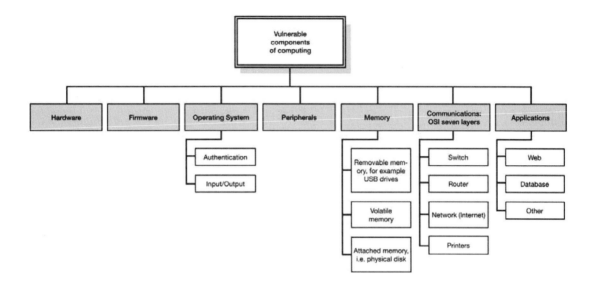

Figure 3-2
Basic Components of Computer Operation

Figure 3-2 shows the basics of computer operation. At the beginning of the computer startup process, the basic instructions for how a computer gets going are stored in its hardware. It has a set of instructions on what to do when it first turns on. This process is referred to as booting up, which is a reference to the concept of a computer pulling itself up by its own bootstraps.

Next the computer begins to read instructions on what to do. The instructions can be stored in a variety of locations, but for the sake of discussion the instruction-storage area can be called firmware. Firmware allows computer instructions to be updated periodically.

After reading those instructions, the computer moves on to the operating system. The operating system, such as Microsoft Windows, Linux, or Mac OS, contains the millions of lines of instructions required to run a modern computer. Among other things, an operating system deals with input and output. That means a user or other agent can input instructions and receive an output in return. In addition, operating systems are typically responsible for user authentication—the process of verifying (authenticating) that the person accessing the device is who he says he is.

The next level of computer system architecture concerns peripherals, items inside or connected to the computer. One example is the hard drive. Typically, the operating system is loaded onto the hard drive, and those instructions are loaded by the computer when it boots. Another peripheral is a CD-ROM drive. During the boot sequence, a computer can take instructions from the CD-ROM drive and act on them. In a number of computer hacking situations, hackers placed specially crafted CD-ROMs with enticing titles like "payroll data" in lunchrooms. A user putting the CD-ROM into his computer has his PC compromised as the CD-ROM executes its startup program.

It is important to note that a computer operates in two primary modes: as a stand-alone computing device and as a device that can communicate with other computers. A computer operates as a stand-alone device by storing and manipulating information in its memory. Memory can contain information that is only available when the computer is on (volatile memory) or information that is available even without power applied to the system (static memory).

Data changes and manipulations are called computations, which occur in a computer's processor. In stand-alone mode, a computer follows a set of instructions to manipulate data, typically via keyboard input, from memory, or from a peripheral. The computer then acts on the data, performing a basic calculation or writing data to memory. This is the basic Turing model of an algorithm.

An original IBM PC in 1981 would not necessarily have been attached to another computer. Thus, one would find it difficult to add or remove anything from the computer without physically accessing it. In that era, securing PCs was easier than it is today. As the 1980s progressed, computers began to speak to one another. Still, even then, much of the work of ISS consisted of securing mainframes inside of data centers.

Regarding computer communications, computers on the Internet communicate via a protocol called Internet Protocol (IP) which is also called TCP/IP (Transport Control Protocol/Internet Protocol). Almost all modern communications via computer follow a model called the Open Systems Interconnect (OSI) Seven Layer Network Model, developed by the International Organization for Standardization. The model (Reed, 2003)

> describes seven layers of interaction for an information system communicating over a network, presenting a stack of layers representing major function areas that are generally required or useful for data communication between nodes in a distributed environment.

The seven layers of the OSI model are as follows:

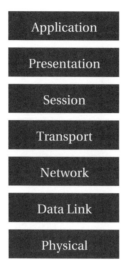

Typically, the list is read from the bottom up.

Layer 1

At the physical layer, computers are communicating by either sending an electrical impulse or not. This level defines the actual voltage and interfaces that a computer uses to communicate.

Layer 2

At the data link level, computers are actually communicating logically. In layer 2 communication, computers can only speak to each other when they can directly contact each other. For one machine to talk to another, the two must be connected. In the simplest form, this can occur when two machines are connected with a wire. In a modern network, cables are run from a computer to a centralized location, typically referred to as an intermediate distribution facility (IDF). In each of these facilities typically sits a switch. The switch is analogous to a telephone switch, in which multiple phones connect and by which one phone can talk to another. In simple terms, every computer directly connected to a switch can speak to any other computer directly connected to the same switch. At this layer, communication happens automatically without additional configuration.

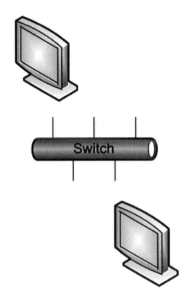

Computers can only directly talk to each other when they can
"see" each other directly.

Figure 3-3
Direct Communication

A person in a room with several other people can typically talk directly to those people. It is easy to talk around a conference room table because one can see the other people in the room. This is like computers connected to the same switch or set of switches. One computer is capable of talking to another computer simply by saying its name.

Switches provide a little privacy, analogous to a whispered conversation between two people sitting next to each other at a conference table. Although a whispered conversation is supposed to be private, there are plenty of ways to overhear it. One could stand close to the people having the conversation or use a specialty microphone. Likewise, in the virtual world hackers can get in the middle of a conversation they are not supposed to be part of. This certainly applies to communication via a local switch. A switch is not only a back-end device that connects computers, but it is also a host that can be configured. It runs programs, meaning it can be compromised (for example, if a cybercriminal gains access to the configuration program).

Layer 3

At the network layer, computers are unable to see each other directly. This is also known as layer 3 communication. This layer was created so machines that could not immediately see each other could still communicate.

For this to occur, it is necessary to have an intermediary that allows for communication to cross many intermediaries in the process. In the physical world, post offices and the phone companies know how to deliver information from one place to another based upon some sort of routing code. The computer device that allows for this to happen is called a router. A router knows how to get from one location to another so computers can talk to each other. Routers also talk to each other so that each router in a critical path knows how to get to another router somewhere else.

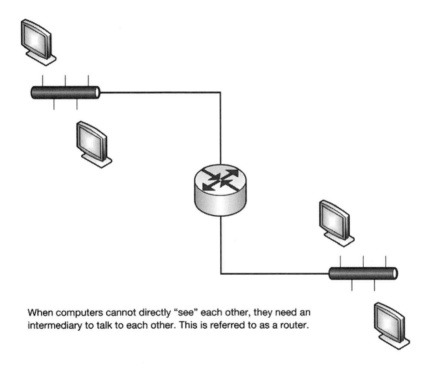

When computers cannot directly "see" each other, they need an intermediary to talk to each other. This is referred to as a router.

Figure 3-4
Communications by Router

Remaining Layers

The other four layers of the OSI model are also important in understanding the way computers interact. For example, the fourth layer, the transport layer, determines the mechanism for how computers are actually going to transport the information between the two computers now that they can talk. The last three layers—session, presentation, and application—address how computers organize data into flows, standardize the data, and perform functions not pertaining directly to network operation.

Also important are the applications that run on a computer that do specific tasks. These can be things like the Web servers that allow users to get access to data, databases that actually maintain data, or something as simple as Microsoft Word. These applications can access data, and it is important to think about how they might be misused.

Data Input Challenges

There are various mechanisms by which someone can access or manipulate information on a computer.

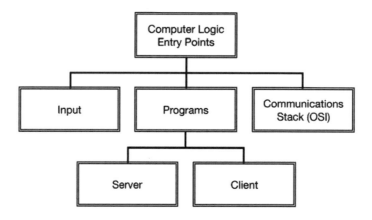

Figure 3-5
Computer Logic Entry Points

A computer typically has three logical entry points for getting it to do something: input, programs, and the communications stack. Input is the easiest means to get information to a computer—one types on a keyboard or uses another input device. Programs, too, are capable of asking the computer to do something. The dangerous part is the communications stack, through which a computer can send input or ask a program to do something from anywhere in the world.

Input comes in many forms. It may consist of typing text into a word processor from the keyboard; it might be a user entering his user name and password; or it might be the computer program controlling the entry/exit system sending an access record to the computer program preventing users who are not in the building from accessing a server containing sensitive information.

One mode of attack via input is to enter unusual text into a log-in field on a Web page, such as "' or 1=1—". If the computer is not prepared to deal appropriately with this input, the computer might return information that the user should not see.

Another category of attack is called buffer overflow. In this instance, a malicious user or program can give more information to the computer program than it is expecting. The extra words or characters can produce a buffer overflow state, giving the computer instructions to do something unintended.

Logic errors can have similar consequences. If the programmer does not write the code correctly, a malicious user can actually get it to do something. Additionally, if the computer assumes something will happen in a certain sequence, but the sequence is disrupted because a program or the network is slow, then something can sneak past the computer and cause a malicious event to happen.

Hosts: It's a Party

A host computer stores information and allows one to manipulate it or communicate with another computer. A host needs a mechanism for taking a command from a user and manipulating the information within it. This is generally referred to as the platform for the computer. In most cases, the platform is one of a limited number of operating systems.

On each of these platforms, one or more application programs can run. One application might be Microsoft Word. Another might be an Internet browser, such as Safari or Internet Explorer. These applications contain millions of lines of instructions. Although each instruction is often very simple, the logical complexity associated with how these instructions interact becomes a breeding ground for error.[13]

---

[13] For example, a simple instruction may say, "Add together the number N1 in storage location S1 and the number N2 in storage location S2 and put the sum in storage location S3." Another simple instruction may say, "Read the number N1 in S1 and execute the instruction N1." The program will get different results depending on what number N1 happens to be stored in S1 at the time the instruction is executed. While instructions like this are very common in programs—and provide the programmer with a great deal of capability—they also are a source of the complexity that lies at the heart of the information systems security challenge.

Any system that is a computer host is potentially compromisable in one way or another, including all of the following systems:

- **Servers.** These are typically machines that serve more than one individual in their specific application. In some cases, when people refer to a host, they are referring to a server, although this is technically inaccurate. Servers are of greater concern because they typically serve more than one person and as a result are usually a repository of data or some mechanism of access to data.

- **Workstations.** These are generally machines that run a standard operating system and on which users can run multiple programs. These classes of machines include desktops and computers with separate CPU devices. Most notably, these machines are not portable. *Workstation* can also mean a high-end desktop computer, but here the term refers to a computer that cannot be moved easily.

- **Laptops.** These are typically identical in function to workstations, but they are portable. They can get into more trouble simply because they can be moved around.

Personal digital assistants (PDAs), such as an iPod Touch, can contain as much information as a computer from the 1990s. Intelligent phones, such as the iPhone or BlackBerry, are also powerful computers. Other devices, such as USB or flash drives, may lack intelligence but still be able to carry data from place to place. MP3 players and digital cameras, too, can carry immense amounts of data.

Anything connected or that can connect to a network is at risk. That now includes phones, cameras, and printers.

Since any device that can communicate with another computer and has memory is referred to as a host, a host could also be a printer, which typically has a Web server as part of its operating system.

Typically, when a user logs onto a host, he needs to be identified and authorized to gain access. This is much the same as going up to a security officer and showing identification. The officer examines the identification badge and a person's face to make a determination that he is who he claims to be. A computer typically identifies a person by asking for a user name and password.

Process for basic login authentication

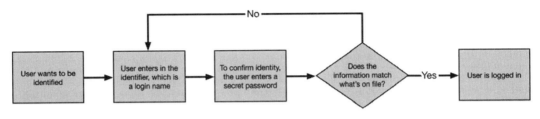

Figure 3-6
Authentication

After identifying a user, the computer checks a database to see what type of authorization that particular user has. The things a user is allowed to do are called rights, permissions, and privileges.

This process of authentication and authorization is part of what is called the AAA triad.[14] The third part of this triad is auditing/accountability, which is an essential part of making sure that what is supposed to be happening is actually happening.

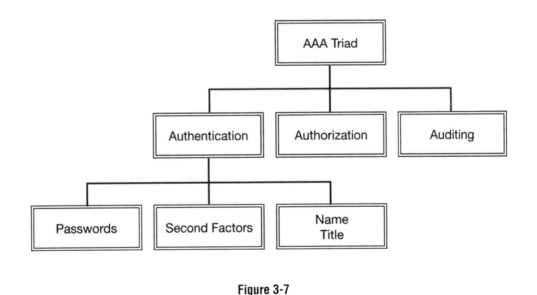

Figure 3-7
AAA Triad

---

[14] More information on the AAA triad can be found at http://datatracker.ietf.org/wg/aaa (Internet Engineering Task Force).

Among the many programs operating on a computer simultaneously are the programs that simply keep the computer going. Called services, these programs run as privileged users, able to do many things on the computer. This creates a problem if someone can get those services to do something undesirable.

The notion of the CIA triad (confidentiality, integrity, and availability) clarifies the types of issues relevant in information security. Figure 3-8 expands on the CIA triad.

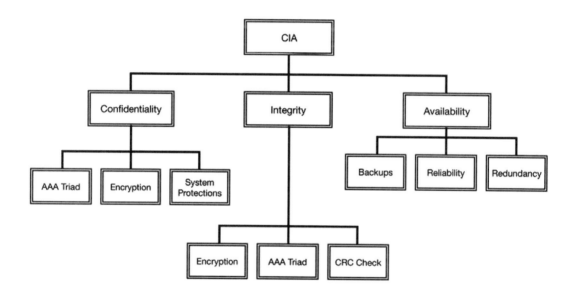

Figure 3-8
CIA Triad, Expanded

Confidentiality

User authentication is critical to making sure people do not get to data which they have no right to access. One mechanism for increasing security is to use an additional authentication factor beyond the user name and password.

Passwords can be guessed, but other authentication mechanisms are much more difficult to guess or copy. One example is biometric authentication, such as fingerprint scanners, hand geometry scanners, or iris scanners. Another mechanism for second-factor authentication is the one time password (OTP) token that either changes when a person presses a button on a device or after a period of time, usually every minute or so.

Another mechanism for ensuring confidentiality is encryption. Unless a person knows how to decrypt the data, he cannot get at it. Encryption comes in many forms and has been used for thousands of years. One of the earliest known methods of encryption is called the Caesar cipher, where individuals use a grid on each end of the encryption method allowing them to move a letter forward a certain number of positions from the actual message. For example, every instance of the letter A could be replaced with the letter M. Modern encryption technologies are far more sophisticated than this. Nevertheless, over time encryption mechanisms are broken, and it is necessary to repeatedly increase the strength of the encryption.

Integrity

Encryption can also help with integrity, because it is very difficult to modify something that one cannot read. Another tool for maintaining integrity is a cyclical redundancy check (CRC), which shows whether data has been tampered with.

Perhaps the most important files whose integrity must be preserved are the files containing user IDs, passwords, and allowed roles (rights, permissions, and privileges.) for all users. An organization would be at the mercy of any cybercriminal able to change such files.

Availability

If users cannot get their data, it is not of much use. An old IT joke says there are two kinds of computer users: those whose hard drives have crashed and those whose hard drives will crash. If data disappears, it is not available. It can also disappear by being stolen. A basic tenet of computing is to back up data off-site, preferably in an appropriate data storage vault. Otherwise, a computer crash, office fire, or other tragedy could leave an organization without its data.

Reliability is a related concern. If a purchased service is not highly reliable, users may not be able to access the service when they need it. If a particular connection to the Internet goes down all the time, workers may not be able to do their jobs.

Redundancy aids the effort to ensure data availability. Computers, mere machines, do break. When designing an information system, it is important to include redundant systems to ensure continuity. For example, if a video recorder server goes down, another video recorder server must be available. Redundancy also requires having a battery backup and generator power in the event of a power outage. Depending on the criticality of the computer system, one may need only enough power to shut down the system or enough to keep the system running. This latter situation may require a generator.

3.2.2 **MANAGING THE IT INFRASTRUCTURE**

After understanding the basic tenets of how computers work and communicate, it is important to understand how they are managed. Security professionals are responsible for the assets of their companies, including assets intertwined with the IT network. They must therefore make sure IT is serving the organization's needs.

One mechanism IT professionals use for managing their work is the IT Infrastructure Library or ITIL (pronounced "eye-til"). This is a framework developed by the British Office of Government Commerce in the 1980s. It has since been adopted as an international standard for managing IT. The standard addresses the concept of a service-level agreement (SLA). This is the way one negotiates with IT professionals for the services an organization needs to have delivered.

Everything an organization desires, from regular to emergency services, must be codified in this way. Otherwise, when something is not working, IT professionals may not be able to meet the organization's needs. For example, if an organization does not specify the appropriate amount of bandwidth needed in both normal and emergency situations, the IT department may not create the appropriate configurations in their equipment to meet these needs. In an active shooter situation, five people might need access to the video server at once. If this need has not been addressed in advance, the necessary resources may not be available when the time comes.

Facilities requirements are also important from the perspective of the IT professional. IT professionals require physical security as well as appropriate environmental controls to make sure their systems are working appropriately. Humidity, vibration, and air conditioning are all important considerations for the IT practitioner. Additionally, physical security practitioners should consult with IT practitioners to make sure that appropriate intrusion detection systems, access control, and video surveillance are in place to protect the physical space around computer-based infrastructure.

This concern includes every place in which users can connect to the network or gain access to servers. If a person gains access to a physical computer or server, he can generally gain access to the data on it. Physical security practitioners should assume that if someone can gain access to the physical switch, he is close to getting to other resources on the network. All these areas must be appropriately secured.

3.2.3 **REAL WORLD COMPUTER SYSTEMS**

The most common type of network connection is to the Internet, and from a logical standpoint, it is the same whether one connects to the Internet from home or from a business. Once traffic enters the open Internet, it is impossible to know who, if anyone, is protecting the data.

Companies have addressed this in a multitude of ways. In some cases, companies pay telecommunications providers for private networks on which only their data travels. Multiple levels of privacy are available, but there are still risks.

One should not trust systems that are not under one's control, so it is prudent to place a device in between the Internet and the systems one needs to protect: a firewall. Firewalls for computers are like firewalls in cars. The intention is to keep a fire away from the inhabitants of the passenger compartment of the car in the event that the engine catches on fire. However, fires can still sometimes break through a firewall.

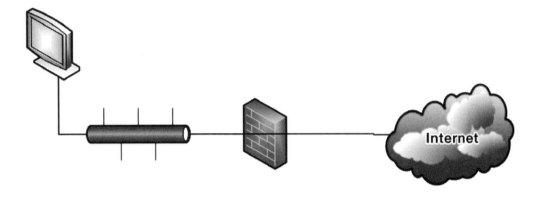

Figure 3-9
Firewall

Firewalls for computers allow only certain traffic to flow from a non-trusted network, like the Internet, to an internal network (where data is typically stored). They should be considered only one tool in the defense-in-depth arsenal.

If a company is truly concerned about the security of its data, over the open Internet or within a more private network, it can use a technology called virtual private network (VPN), which encrypts data from one point to another. For the data to be compromised, assuming the use of an adequate encryption algorithm, somebody has to know the secrets used to encrypt the data.

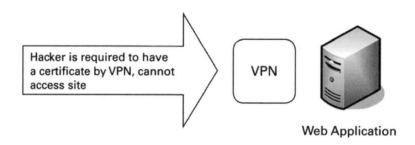

Figure 3-10
Virtual Private Network

An important issue in ISS is cloud computing, which enables companies to offer services without an investment in technology infrastructure. One appeal is that many IT concerns are managed by someone else. Unfortunately, cloud computing also raises data protection concerns.

Real Vulnerabilities: An E-Mail Example

E-mail has become the de facto standard communication mechanism in the corporate arena. Most interestingly, e-mail is directly available to the Internet. Someone can send e-mail directly to another person's mail server, and that mail server delivers it to the second person. In general, this is good; people like getting e-mail because it connects them to other people efficiently.

However, to do its job, mail software must have a certain amount of permission on the recipient's server. A specially crafted e-mail can get the mail system to do something undesirable (to the recipient). Such "escalation of privilege" attacks succeed because the e-mail program is tricked into executing the e-mail as if it were a program rather than simply processing it as text.[15]

This type of attack is nowhere more prevalent than in Web applications. Just like physical security professionals, ISS professionals apply defense in depth to protect assets. The more layers someone must penetrate to attack a target, the less likely he is to succeed in the attack.

Web applications generally make such attacks much easier. Users on the Internet announce their presence, making data available. That is fine when the right user is at his own bank's Web site. However, risks abound.

User names and passwords are only good if they are secret and not able to be guessed. The first thing a hacker can look for is someone's user name. Often it is guessable, perhaps an e-mail address. It is a slightly more difficult task to either guess the password or use a program called a brute force password hack to go through common permutations of passwords. One must assume that a cybercriminal can penetrate these two defenses, user names and passwords.

Typical office applications like Microsoft Word or Apple Pages generally seem benign. However, in some cases, individuals have been able to send files that tell those programs to do things they should not do. A user clicks on that file in an e-mail or downloads it via a Web page, with permission or not, and an attack is under way.

Some people like to use a service called file transfer protocol (FTP) to share files. Unfortunately, this is another mechanism by which others can access one's computer. Programs do what they are told, at best, and unless properly specified and implemented—a very challenging task—they don't know right from wrong.

Related Peripherals

Several computer peripherals are of concern to the physical security practitioner. Already mentioned are the many portable devices that can store data, such as external hard drives, flash drives, iPhones, etc. These devices can both load malicious software and take away data that should not be taken away.

---

[15] A simple corollary to the main result in Turing's 1936 paper is that there is no algorithm for distinguishing between program and data.

The printer, perhaps the oldest form of communication that connects to a computer network, is also of concern. Printers are connected to the network, so communications to and from them can be intercepted. Furthermore, some printers contain hard drives or on-board memory, which must be wiped when printing confidential information. Finally, the hard copy that printers create can be taken from one place to another. It is essential to make sure an organization's printers are secured and placed in appropriate locations.

Modern copiers are now referred to as multifunction devices, which can fax, scan, print, and copy. Security professionals should consider whether data on these devices could be removed, in the form of hard drives or memory, and used for the wrong reason. Scanning is another concern for the security practitioner because it converts hard copy documents into an electronic format that can be sent across the world in seconds. Every device connected to the network can have an adverse effect.

Telecommunications

Telecommunication systems are critical to business and personal life. While most of these systems are still based on older technologies, new technologies have changed the landscape of telecommunications concerns.

While considered old by modern standards and named legacy systems by IT professionals, private branch exchange (PBX) systems are still complex computerized devices that can be compromised. A PBX is the central core of many corporate telephone systems. A multitude of features must be understood to make sure they are protected. These include voicemail, domestic and international long-distance, call forwarding, call conferencing, call monitoring, and a host of other features.

Additionally, some numbers, such as the traditional 976 numbers, charge a fee when called, so they must be blocked. The phone carrier can make sure such numbers cannot be charged to the organization's account.

Traditional PBX systems connect to the international phone system using one or more different technologies. These technologies are analogous to Internet connections that go to the central office. The central office acts on commands issued by the PBX. This is one more place where security can be compromised.

Phone systems are like any other computer system. They are simply proprietary operating systems either running on an embedded system burned into hardware or on top of a computer server, like any other application. All features, including passwords to voicemail, long-distance dialing, and call monitoring, should be treated identically to any other computer system.

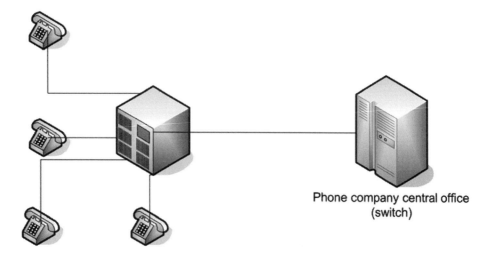

In a traditional PBX system, phones are directly connected to
the PBX, which is directly connected to the phone company
central office.

Figure 3-11
Traditional PBX System

Most legacy phone systems do not actually sit on the network. Systems that bridge legacy
and modern voice-over-IP (VOIP) phone systems may sit on the network, but they are less
prevalent. Such systems often have a remote maintenance and administration terminal
(RMAT) that can be used to dial into the system and make configuration changes to it.
Additionally, legacy phone systems can turn on auditing to help track costs and detect fraud.

Each phone in a legacy PBX system is connected directly to the PBX. In most systems, this is
done via a digital connection, but it can also be via plain old telephone service (POTS). A
POTS telephone line is an old-fashioned, two-pair phone line that is connected via copper
from the phone to the central office (CO). POTS lines are also referred to as analog lines,
which are required for fire systems in most jurisdictions and are a good idea for intrusion
detection alarm connections.

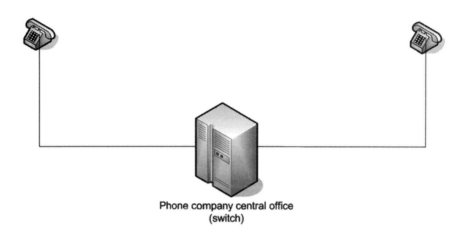

Figure 3-12
Phone Company Central Office

Telephone calling cards have also significantly declined in cost over the last 20 years. Still, if they are compromised, for example by being seen over a user's shoulder, the user may end up with a larger bill than expected. Many companies are now using prepaid calling cards to mitigate the risk of receiving large, unexpected bills.

A newer player is the fully computerized, fully redundant VOIP system. Converging phones onto the network has many benefits: it is less expensive because the wiring is the same as for a computer; one can more easily move a phone from one location to another because it behaves like a computer; and because the systems all behave like computers, IT personnel are more capable of managing them. Additionally, these systems typically have far more advanced features than the older, legacy systems. They can also use advanced technologies to reduce telephone costs significantly.

However, VOIP systems are completely accessible on the network. That means every phone and every server hosting phone-related information, including voicemail and the actual phone calls in progress, have the potential to be compromised.

A typical modern phone system has a server that manages the process of getting the voice from the phone one talks on, which is really another host, out to the traditional phone system and to another phone. As Figure 3-13 shows, voice traffic from the phone to the phone company central office travels in part over a network.

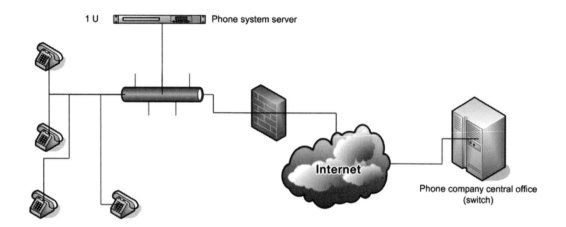

In a Voice-over-IP system, each phone is a host, as is the device which controls the phone system. Traffic flows on the user's network, and possibly the Internet, before getting to the phone company.

Figure 3-13
Voice-over-IP (VOIP) System

Additionally, to save money some companies connect to their central office via the Internet, meaning there is additional exposure of the system to potential compromise. Moreover, the phone system itself, including the additional components, is available on the network and could be potentially compromised through various network-based attacks, including attacks originating from the Internet. This risk affects such services as voicemail and dialing via a soft phone operated on one's computer, as well as contact information. All these concerns must be considered in ISS policies.

In a traditional phone system, all the power comes from the PBX out to the phones, and home phones get their power from the phone company. Security professionals should make sure that, in the event of a power outage, the critical paths for phone data have backup power for 12 hours or more, the typical expectation of a modern phone system.

It is also necessary to ensure redundancy across all the necessary components for keeping the phone system up. A legacy PBX is typically built sturdily with few moving parts, such as hard drives, fans, etc. A VOIP phone system typically runs on regular computers, which are more prone to failure than a simple solid-state device. A professional VOIP installation typically has two of these machines in a redundant configuration so that if one fails, the other can take over.

The need for redundancy extends to the routers that connect to the phone system, the lines that connect to the phone system, and the switches that connect all the networks together. Physical security practitioner should plan for different emergency scenarios. For example, in a building that does not allow cell phone usage, what would happen if there were no phones available to call 911?

Several new technologies that come along with modern phone systems can greatly enhance the productivity and safety of an organization's phones. E911, for example, can tell the emergency responder exactly what location in a building called 911. Integrating this technology with the organization's security operations center can help site security staff handle emergencies better. Other modern phone system features include integrated public address systems, automated systems for sending out messages, and the ability to log into other systems via the phone.

Another phone-related issue is faxing. Traditional faxing security centered on who was on hand to receive the fax and whether it was going to the right person. For example, sending a fax to a public reception area, such as a hotel, makes that fax no longer confidential. However, modern fax systems come with other concerns. First, some modern fax machines have memory that stores fax images. That memory may or may not be appropriately wiped when the fax has been transmitted. Second, more and more systems can transmit and receive faxes electronically, complicating security. For example, in states where confidential information must be encrypted, confidential faxes must be encrypted as well. Additionally, users must take special precautions to protect faxes; previously they were simply printed, and now they are available electronically.

Cell phones and PDAs further complicate the telecommunication situation. As portable devices, they present two types of risk. First, someone may eavesdrop on the conversation. In 2009, the algorithm used to encrypt most consumer phones was broken (O'Brien, 2009). Physical security practitioners certainly must be concerned about security on wireless communications. Smartphones raise even greater concerns. Enormous amounts of sensitive data, which used to be contained within the perimeter of a company's network, may now reside on a small, permanently mobile, easy-to-lose device.

3.2.4 ADDITIONAL INFORMATION SECURITY CONCEPTS

Quality of Service

Another critical concept is quality of service (QoS). On a computer network, many different devices are vying for attention and the ability to communicate. Time-sensitive information, such as data from video cameras, must be able to get through under any circumstances. After a security professional identifies which data on a network is critical, network administrators can tell the network to give the data priority.

Third-Party Review

Third-party review is a critical aspect of any information security program. Basically, an organization is not indemnified by outsourcing any particular element of its information security or information technology programs. Each organization is responsible for managing its vendors and ensuring that they come up to a specific level, typically at least the same as the contracting organization, in their information security practices.

The Payment Card Industry Data Security Standard (PCI DSS) notes the following (PCI Security Standards Council, 2010, p. 11):

> For those entities that outsource storage, processing, or transmission of cardholder data to third-party service providers, [the entity] must document the role of each service provider, clearly identifying which requirements apply to the reviewed entity and which apply to the service provider. There are two options for third-party service providers to validate compliance: 1) They can undergo a PCI DSS assessment on their own and provide evidence to their customers to demonstrate their compliance, or 2) If they do not undergo their own PCI DSS assessment, they will need to have their services reviewed during the course of each of their customer's PCI DSS assessments.

In an extranet policy template from SANS, a noted authority on information security, the following are appropriate courses of action when allowing third-party access to an organization's data (2006):

- a security review of the third party in question by the information security department
- a business case for having the data access
- an agreement of the requirements for the access
- reexamination of the security in place at the third party when changes occur

Additionally, it is prudent to include periodic review of all external access to data, including the right to audit the third party.

3.2.5 **INFORMATION SECURITY TECHNOLOGIES**

The following is a brief overview of selected information security technologies:

Intrusion detection system (IDS)

An intrusion detection system monitor one's network and attempts to decipher either via behavior or patterns/signatures whether someone is trying to attack the system. A variation of the IDS is an intrusion prevention system (IPS), which is designed to automatically stop an attack in progress. However, an IPS may stop a valid service, unnecessarily preventing users from accessing the network.

Host intrusion protection system (HIPS)

This is like an IDS except that it operates on a host system, such as a computer or server. HIPS is an evolution of host protection from antivirus, because it is able to look at both signatures and behavior to protect a machine. When people claim antivirus software is dead, they mean that programmers cannot write signatures fast enough to identify and keep out the onslaught of viruses, worms, or Trojan threats and that behavior-based protection is needed.

Certificates

A certificate is a mechanism by which individuals who do not know each other can ensure a secure transaction. Certificates are asymmetric tools that work like a lock and key, allowing individuals to exchange information securely over a non-trusted channel. Certificates are also used frequently to enable encryption, because by using a certificate pair, it is possible to pass a shared secret used to decrypt the data. Because certificates are typically slow at encrypting data, it is preferable to use the certificate simply to exchange the secret and then to use a much faster algorithm for exchanging data.

Security information and event manager (SIEM)

A SIEM is a device that looks at all the log activity on a network and attempts to point out what is most important to facilitate response to incursions and other problems on the network. There is now a class of software for the physical security realm that does the same thing, called a physical security information manager (PSIM).

E-mail gateway

This is a device that looks at inbound and outbound e-mail to determine whether it is a security risk. One purpose of an e-mail gateway is to reduce the amount of spam, or unwanted e-mail, that comes into a network. A large amount of spam can have malware, and gateway systems makes it possible to reduce the threat.

Web gateway/proxy server

Web gateways and proxy servers filter which Web pages can be downloaded. They may keep users from accessing particular sites, such as pornographic sites, or work as a proxy, or intermediary, that removes pages that might have malicious content.

Data loss protection (DLP)

This technology keeps people from sending certain data, such as trade secrets or other intellectual property, off the network, either inadvertently or on purpose.

Web application firewall (WAF)

A WAF is a special-purpose device that filters traffic before it hits an organization's Web site. WAFs are used to block malicious attacks on vulnerable code from reaching their target, specifically on a Web server.

Network access control (NAC)

NAC is a technology by which computers are not admitted to a network unless they are allowed, do not have any malicious software, and meet the standards of the network.

802.1x

This is an Institute of Electrical and Electronics Engineers (IEEE) standard that allows for specific authentication before a computer can come onto a network. It is often used with network access control.

Common Vulnerabilities and Exposures (CVE)

This is an on-line dictionary of publicly known information security vulnerabilities and exposures. It forms the backbone of the National Vulnerability Database and is an essential tool in the twin disciplines of vulnerability management and patch management. It is available at http://cve.mitre.org.

3.3   **ISS PRACTITIONER FRAMEWORKS**

ISS is sufficiently complex to require a systematic framework if one is to ensure that countermeasures are adequate to manage the risk. A security framework organizes the ISS body of knowledge in a strategically sound and focused way that supports both planning and action.

Several ISS practitioner perspectives are in use. They have been developed by different organizations, and each tends to reflect a different point of view. By gaining exposure to multiple points of view, the security professional is better able to understand the full range of challenges and solutions in ISS.

Each of these perspectives deals at an abstract level with the question of standards for the protection of information system assets. Their points of view are quite different, as is their pedigree.

- ISO/IEC 27001:2005 and ISO/IEC 27002:2005 are extensions of ISO 17799, which originated in Australia and Great Britain before being adopted by the International Organization for Standardization.

- The CISSP Common Body of Knowledge was developed to characterize the body of knowledge required for certification as an ISS professional. It was developed by ISSA and is managed by (ISC)^2.

- *Guidance for Boards of Directors and Executive Management* was developed and published by the Information Systems Audit and Control Association.

- "Generally Accepted Information System Security Practices" are being developed by an international consortium under the leadership of ISSA, with the majority of participants coming from the United States.

3.3.1   **ISO/IEC 27001:2005 and ISO/IEC 27002:2005**

These two standards, known informally as ISO 27001 and 27002, form an emerging international standard for managing information security. They are the first acknowledged worldwide standards to identify a code of practice for the management of information security.

Together the standards identify 11 specific vital information security management practices, integrating them into a framework called an information security management system (ISMS). An organization's information is secure only to the extent that these 11 practices are being systematically managed and strengthened via the ISMS. Weaknesses in any single practice or in the ISMS itself can negate the combined strength of the other practices.

The centerpiece of ISO 27001 is its concept of an ISMS. An organization's ISMS is that part of the organization's (p.2)

> overall management system, based on a business risk approach, to establish, implement, operate, monitor, review and improve information security. ... The management system includes organizational structure, policies, planning activities, responsibilities, practices, procedures, processes and resources.

The 11 information security management practices are as follows:

- security policy

- organization of information security

- asset management

- human resources security

- physical and environmental security

- communications and operations management

- access control

- information systems acquisition, development and maintenance

- information security incident management

- business continuity management

- compliance

3.3.2 CISSP COMMON BODY OF KNOWLEDGE

Just as ISO 27001 and ISO 27002 provide definitive certification guidance for an organization, the Certified Information Systems Security Professional (CISSP) body of knowledge provides definitive certification requirements appropriate to the individual ISS professional. CISSP is the de facto standard for ISS certification. The CISSP Common Body of Knowledge organizes ISS into 10 domains, listed below, followed by a brief discussion of each:

- **Access control.** Access control is defined by the AAA triad, authentication, authorization, and accountability (sometimes termed auditing). The fact that an entire section is devoted to access control indicates the importance of this basic principle of information security.

- **Application development security.** A key tenet in information security is the need to write secure code. That means the programming instructions given to the computer must do what they're supposed to do and not respond incorrectly to commands.

- **Business continuity and disaster recovery planning.** According to Gregg (2009, p. 280):

  > The business continuity plan (BCP) and disaster recovery plan (DRP) domain address the need to prepare for, and how to respond to, the occasions when things do go wrong. For a company to be successful under duress of hardship or catastrophe, it must plan how to preserve business operations in the face of these major disruptions.

- **Cryptography.** Cryptography is an important aspect of information security, as it prevents individuals from gaining access to the actual data (Gregg, 2009, p. 118):

  > Cryptography is concerned with the ways in which information can be encoded or encrypted to prevent disclosure. It is tied closely to three basic pillars of security: integrity, nonrepudiation, and confidentiality.

- **Information security governance and risk management.** The section deals with how an organization manages information security by specifically identifying risks and dealing with them through policies, procedures, and guidelines.

- **Legal, regulations, investigations, and compliance.** These concerns are a major part of information security. Additionally, knowing the elements of conducting a forensic computer investigation is important for the information security practitioner.

- **Operations security.** According to Gregg (2009, p. 450):

  > Readers preparing for the ISC2 Certified Information Systems Security Professional exam and those reviewing the operational security domain must know resources that should be protected; principles of best practices, methods to restrict access, potential abuses of access, selection of appropriate controls, and response to attacks.

- **Physical (environmental) security:** Obviously, physical security is second nature to physical security practitioners. The goal is to keep people from actually physically accessing electronic devices and to maintain an appropriate environment in which the systems can run.

- **Security architecture and design.** This section specifically deals with hardware, software, security controls, and documentation. It is important to understand how systems work and to architect them appropriately so they behave as expected.

- **Telecommunications and network security.** This section is analogous to the previous discussion of how computers communicate and how to secure the network over which they communicate.

For physical security practitioners interested in learning more about information security, the CISSP is an excellent place to start. It provides a broad-based knowledge of the tenets of information security.

3.3.3 INFORMATION SECURITY GOVERNANCE: GUIDANCE FOR BOARDS OF DIRECTORS AND EXECUTIVE MANAGEMENT

The third perspective, provided in *Information Security Governance: Guidance for Boards of Directors and Executive Management* (ISACA, 2001), represents the point of view of those responsible for auditing the maturity level of an organization's ISS.

ISACA's model was built on a software engineering management maturity framework that had been developed in the 1980s by the Software Engineering Institute, a national technology center at Carnegie Mellon University. The model measures the extent to which information security is formally and proactively managed throughout the organization.

Organizations can apply ISACA's management maturity model to their own organization as a

- snapshot-in-time assessment tool, helping the organization identify the relative strengths of its information security management practices,

- tool for identifying an appropriate security management maturity level, to which the organization can evolve,

- method for identifying the gaps between its current security maturity level and its desired level,

- tool for planning and managing an organization-wide information security management improvement program for systematically improving the organization's information security management capabilities, and a

- tool for planning and managing specific information security improvement projects.

Figure 3-14 provides an overview of each information security management maturity level.

Management Maturity Level	Description
0	*Security management is nonexistent* The organization does not manage the security of information assets
1	*Initial ad hoc security management* Security management is ad hoc and not organized; management responsibility is fragmented or nonexistent
2	*Repeatable but intuitive security management* Basic security countermeasures and processes are implemented; management responsibility, authority, and accountability are assigned
3	*Defined process* Security management flows from organizational strategy and from an organization-wide risk management policy; employees receive regular training and education
4	*Managed and measurable* Security management is monitored and measured; regular feedback is used to assess and improve management effectiveness
5	*Security management is optimized* Information security configuration guides are followed

Figure 3-14
Information Security Management Maturity Level

The major benefit of the ISACA framework is that it allows for maturity levels, making it possible to measure how well an organization is doing compared to how well it could do.

3.3.4 GENERALLY ACCEPTED INFORMATION SYSTEM SECURITY PRACTICES (GAISP)

The fourth perspective comes from the draft standard of "Generally Accepted Information System Security Practices" (GAISP) under development by the Information Systems Security Association (ISSA). It is notable for codifying real-world ISS practices encompassing both the management and delivery of ISS capabilities.

GAISP is an ongoing project to collect and document information security principles that have been proven in practice and accepted by practitioners. GAISP draws on established security guidance and standards to create comprehensive, objective guidance for information security professionals, organizations, governments, and users. The use of existing, accepted documents and standards is designed to ensure a high level of acceptance for the final GAISP product.

3.4 THE EMERGING LEGAL, REGULATORY, AND CONTRACTUAL LANDSCAPE REGARDING ISS

In addition to understanding the ISS practitioner frameworks, security professionals should be aware of the emerging body of information security laws and regulations. The legal framework is generally designed to obligate organizations to protect sensitive information in its care belonging to others. This section examines the following legal topics:

- Payment Card Industry Data Security Standard
- Health Care and Insurance Portability and Accountability Act
- Gramm-Leach-Bliley Act
- Children's Online Privacy Protection Act
- Sarbanes-Oxley Act
- Red Flag Rules
- FTC enforcement actions
- state breach-disclosure and related ISS and privacy laws
- European Union Data Protection Directive
- emerging case law

3.4.1 PAYMENT CARD INDUSTRY DATA SECURITY STANDARD (PCI DSS)

The Payment Card Industry Data Security Standard is a worldwide information security standard defined by the Payment Card Industry Security Standards Council (2010). With origins in the separate ISS programs of Visa, MasterCard, American Express, Discover, and JCB International, the standard is designed to provide a uniform set of ISS standards for protecting credit card information. The standard applies to all organizations that hold, process, or exchange cardholder information from any card branded with the logo of one of the preceding companies.

The standard contains 12 requirements organized into six broad categories. Included are requirements for security management, policies, and procedures. The PCI DSS is structured as follows (pp. 2-3):

Build and Maintain a Secure Network

- Requirement 1: Install and maintain a firewall configuration to protect cardholder data.

- Requirement 2: Do not use vendor-supplied defaults for system passwords and other security parameters.

Protect Cardholder Data

- Requirement 3: Protect stored cardholder data.

- Requirement 4: Encrypt transmission of cardholder data across open, public networks.

Maintain a Vulnerability Management Program

- Requirement 5: Use and regularly update antivirus software or programs.

- Requirement 6: Develop and maintain secure systems and applications.

Implement Strong Access Control Measures

- Requirement 7: Restrict access to cardholder data by business need to know.

- Requirement 8: Assign a unique ID to each person with computer access.

- Requirement 9: Restrict physical access to cardholder data.

Regularly Monitor and Test Networks

- Requirement 10: Track and monitor all access to network resources and cardholder data.

- Requirement 11: Regularly test security systems and processes.

Maintain an Information Security Policy

- Requirement 12: Maintain a policy that addresses information security for employees and contractors.

Failure to meet the standard comes with serious consequences. In January 2010, Heartland Payment Systems agreed to pay $60 million as part of a settlement agreement with Visa. Earlier Heartland settled with American Express for $3.6 million. Still to come are settlements with MasterCard and Discover. The payments are the result of a 2008 breach when cybercriminals stole credit card information of millions of credit card holders (Cordeiro, 2010).

3.4.2 **HEALTH CARE AND INSURANCE PORTABILITY AND ACCOUNTABILITY ACT (HIPAA)**

HIPAA was one of the first significant attempts to adopt a standard of care for electronic transactions in the health care field. While much of HIPAA addresses the rights of patients under the health insurance plans, HIPAA also includes key provisions relating to patients' privacy rights. Insurance companies, doctors, hospitals, laboratories, and employers who maintain employee health plans are subject to HIPAA provisions.

HIPAA has been significantly expanded and amended by the adoption of the Health Information Technology for Economic and Clinical Health (HITECH) Act in 2009. Among other things, the HITECH Act requires that business associates of covered entities also adopt specific security measures.

The U.S. Department of Health and Human Services (HHS) has issued regulations providing for the protection of the privacy of "individually identifiable health information" created, received, or otherwise in the possession of entities covered by HIPAA (45 CFR 160, 162, 164).

HIPAA information security regulations require covered entities and business associates to do the following to protect such information (45 CFR 162):

- Maintain a risk-driven information security management program based on a combination of administrative, technical, and physical controls.

- Ensure the confidentiality, integrity, and availability of all electronic protected health information the covered entity creates, receives, maintains, or transmits.

- Protect against any reasonably anticipated threats or hazards to the security or integrity of such information.

- Protect against any reasonably anticipated uses or disclosures of such information that are not permitted or otherwise required.

- Ensure compliance by its work force.

- Ensure compliance by third parties with whom information is shared.

HIPAA illustrates the general trend requiring an organization to proactively manage the security of information entrusted to it.

The HITECH Act and associated regulations published by HHS and the Federal Trade Commission require covered entities, business associates, and other entities that host health care records to disclose to patients—and regulatory agencies—the occurrence of a breach of security that affect protected health information in paper or electronic form.

3.4.3 GRAMM-LEACH-BLILEY ACT (GLBA)

In 1999 Congress passed the Gramm-Leach-Bliley Act, which regulates the use and disclosure of nonpublic personal information about individuals who obtain financial products or services from financial institutions (15 USC 6801):

> It is the policy of the Congress that each financial institution has an affirmative and continuing obligation to respect the privacy of its customers and to protect the security and confidentiality of those customers' nonpublic personal information.

> In furtherance of the policy ... each agency or authority ... shall establish appropriate standards for the financial institutions subject to their jurisdiction relating to administrative, technical, and physical safeguards

> (1) to insure the security and confidentiality of customer records and information;

> (2) to protect against any anticipated threats or hazards to the security or integrity of such records; and

> (3) to protect against unauthorized access to or use of such records or information which could result in substantial harm or inconvenience to any customer

GLBA, on the surface, applies only to financial institutions. However, the broad definitions in GLBA mean that it applies not only to banks and other traditional financial institutions but also to a wide variety of firms and individuals that assist in effecting financial transactions. These include broker/dealers, investment advisors, mortgage lenders, payday lenders, finance companies, mortgage brokers, account servicers, check cashers, wire transferors, travel agencies operated in connection with financial services, collection agencies, credit counselors and other financial advisors, tax preparation firms, and non-federally insured credit unions.

GLBA generally prohibits a financial institution from disclosing nonpublic personal information to a nonaffiliated third party, either directly or through an affiliate, unless the institution has disclosed to the customer, in a clear and conspicuous manner, that the information may be disclosed to a third party; has given the consumer an opportunity to direct that the information not be disclosed; and has described the manner in which the consumer can exercise the nondisclosure option.

Financial institutions must also prepare and promulgate privacy statements that describe the institution's policies with regard to disclosing nonpublic personal information to affiliates and nonaffiliated third parties; disclosing nonpublic personal information of persons who have ceased to be customers of the institution; and the categories of nonpublic personal information the institution collects. The institution is required to disclose clearly and conspicuously those policies and practices at the time that it establishes a customer relationship and not less than annually during the continuation of the customer relationship. This has resulted in an avalanche of paper from banks, brokerage houses, accountants, and others who provide financial services.

GLBA also regulates what steps a business must take to prevent the unintentional sharing of nonpublic personal information in its computer systems. Each federal and state agency with GLBA jurisdiction has separate information security safeguard regulations.[16] Although none are identical, they generally emphasize the following:

- executive management involvement
- risk- and vulnerability-driven measures, based on regular assessments
- written information security policies
- employee training
- control of third parties

A spillover effect of GLBA is increased enforcement activity by the Federal Trade Commission. Additionally, many of the industries directly affected by GLBA are beginning to apply the standards imposed on them to their clients. For example, insurance companies are beginning to review privacy statements and policies of their insureds, and banks are beginning to consider these issues in their underwriting decisions.

Numerous regulations that have significant security implications apply to financial institutions. For example, special rules require financial institutions to use two-factor authentication in order to identify users of their on-line services. Other regulations define the steps that financial institutions must take in the event of a breach of security.

3.4.4 CHILDREN'S ONLINE PRIVACY PROTECTION ACT (COPPA)

COPPA (effective April 21, 2000) applies to any on-line operator that collects personal information from children under 13. The rules adopted under COPPA spell out what a Web site operator must include in a privacy policy, when and how to seek verifiable consent from a parent, and what responsibilities an operator has to protect a child's privacy and safety on-line. In addition to creating challenges for the design of Web sites—for example, many Web operators have redesigned their sites to make them less appealing to children under 13— COPPA and the rules that implement it impose requirements for privacy notices and create specific procedures that must be followed before an operator may obtain information from

---

[16] For example, 12 CFR 30 (Office of the Comptroller of the Currency); 12 CFR 208, 211, 225, 263, (Board of Governors of the Federal Reserve System); 12 CFR 308, 364 (Federal Deposit Insurance Corporation); 12 CFR 568, 570 (Office of Thrift Supervision); 16 CFR 314 (Federal Trade Commission); and 17 CFR 248 (Securities and Exchange Commission).

children. COPPA has caused many businesses (and should spur all businesses) to consider their privacy policies, both in form and substance, and develop practice guidelines.

The Federal Trade Commission enforces COPPA. Some of the fines it has imposed include the following :[17]

- $100,000 fine against Mrs. Fields

- $85,000 fine against Hershey Foods

- $1,000,000 fine against social networking site Xanga.com

- $75,000 fine against Bonzi Software

- $130,000 fine against social network site Imbee.com

- $1,000,000 fine against Sony BMG Music

- $250,000 fine against Iconix Brand

3.4.5 SARBANES-OXLEY ACT (SOX)

The Sarbanes-Oxley Law of 2002 (SOX) has been called the most significant new securities law since the Securities and Exchange Commission was created in 1934. SOX places substantial additional responsibilities on officers and directors of public companies and imposes significant criminal penalties on chief executive officers (CEOs), chief financial officers (CFOs), and others who violate its provisions.

The new requirements under SOX transforms the way all public companies are managed from top to bottom. Even corporations that are not public today, but hope to become publicly owned or be sold to a public company in the future, need to be aware of the basic requirements for operating a company in compliance with SOX, particularly the requirements for establishing, following, and disclosing internal controls and procedures. The requirements obligate all public companies to address their information security procedures and practices in a very public way.

Section 404 of SOX requires the management of a public company to assess the effectiveness of the company's internal control over financial reporting. Section 404 also requires management to include in the company's annual report to shareholders management's conclusion from that assessment. Section 404 has the most relevance to information security with its requirement that management develop, document, test, and monitor its internal controls and its disclosure controls and procedures.

---

[17] Details regarding each fine are available at http://www.ftc.gov/opa.

The most significant new responsibility faced by the CEO and CFO of every public company is the required personal certification of the company's annual and quarterly reports. To meet the certification requirements regarding the internal controls and disclosure controls, the SEC recommends that every company establish a disclosure committee consisting of the CFO, controller, heads of divisions, and other persons having significant responsibility for the company's principal operating divisions. The disclosure committee should review the company's existing internal controls and disclosure controls and procedures, document them, evaluate their adequacy, correct any material weaknesses, and create monitoring and testing procedures that will be used every quarter to continuously evaluate the company's internal controls and disclosure controls and procedures.

While SOX was adopted in response to perceived inadequacies and misconduct by corporate officers and directors, its focus on systems and the certification of the adequacy of reporting schemes has had a broad effect on the establishment of corporate controls and standards. These changes do not exist in a vacuum; principles of corporate governance that first applied to public corporations have often been extended to private companies, sometimes through state law and regulation, other times through market forces (such as when auditors and insurance carriers adopt similar standards for public and nonpublic companies).

3.4.6 RED FLAG RULES

The Red Flags Rule implement Sections 114 and 315 the Fair and Accurate Credit Transaction (FACT) Act. Different versions of the Red Flags Rule have been adopted by the various agencies that regulate financial institutions, as well as the Federal Trade Commission (FTC).[18] For example, 16 CFR 681 (FTC) requires

> each ... creditor that holds any consumer account, or other account for which there is a reasonably foreseeable risk of identity theft, to develop and implement an Identity Theft Prevention Program (Program) for combating identity theft.
>
> The Program must include reasonable policies and procedures for detecting, preventing, and mitigating identity theft and enable a ... creditor to:
>
> 1. Identify relevant patterns, practices, and specific forms of activity that are "red flags" signaling possible identity theft and incorporate those red flags into the Program;
>
> 2. Detect red flags that have been incorporated into the Program;

---

[18] For example: 12 CFR 41 (Comptroller of the Currency); 12 CFR 222 (Federal Reserve Board); 12 CFR 334 and 364 (Federal Deposit Insurance Corporation); 12 CFR 571 (Office of Thrift Supervision); 12 CFR 717 (National Credit Union Association); and 16 CFR 681 (Federal Trade Commission).

3. Respond appropriately to any red flags that are detected to prevent and mitigate identity theft; and

4. Ensure the Program is updated periodically to reflect changes in risks from identity theft.

The purpose of the program is the early detection and prevention of identity theft.

"Covered Accounts" Require Protection

According to FTC regulations, a "covered account" means either of two things:

> An account that a financial institution or creditor offers or maintains, primarily for personal, family, or household purposes, that involves or is designed to permit multiple payments or transactions, such as a credit card account, mortgage loan, automobile loan, margin account, cell phone account, utility account, checking account, or savings account; and

> Any other account that the financial institution or creditor offers or maintains for which there is a reasonably foreseeable risk to customers or to the safety and soundness of the financial institution or creditor from identity theft, including financial, operational, compliance, reputation, or litigation risks.

Red Flag Categories

Red flags that must be identified, detected, and responded to include the following:

- alerts, notifications, or warnings from a consumer reporting agency

- suspicious documents

- suspicious personally identifying information, such as a suspicious address

- unusual use of—or suspicious activity relating to—a covered account

- notices from customers, victims of identity theft, law enforcement authorities, or other businesses about possible identity theft in connection with covered accounts

3.4.7 FTC ENFORCEMENT ACTIONS

The Federal Trade Commission has been at the forefront of privacy and information security regulations. In that role, it has adopted a "safeguards rule" under the GBLA, which requires each financial institution within its jurisdiction to (16 CFR 314)

> develop, implement, and maintain a comprehensive information security program that is written in one or more readily accessible parts and contains administrative, technical, and physical safeguards that are appropriate to your size and complexity, the nature and scope of your activities, and the sensitivity of any customer information at issue.

Under its authority to protect consumers, the FTC is in a position to adopt regulations that cross the boundaries of all industries. It also requires each business within the jurisdiction of the FTC to make determinations that are consistent with the size and complexity of the business and its activities, as well as a sensitivity of customer information at issue. It does not provide specific rules; it require that businesses regulate themselves. Companies are thus forced to analyze their operations, needs, and vulnerabilities to comply with the FTC's GLBA safeguards rule.

Another FTC tool to address privacy or security violations has been the application of Section 5 of the FTC Act, which prohibits unfair and deceptive practices. This law has been used in enforcement actions against a wide variety of businesses, including Tower Records, DSW Warehouse, Microsoft, Eli Lilly, and CVS Caremark. Under the FTC Act, the FTC is directed to prevent unfair methods of competition and unfair or deceptive acts or practices in or affecting commerce. At its Web site, the FTC highlights its intention to regulate on-line privacy as part of its privacy initiative:[19]

> A key part of the Commission's privacy program is making sure companies keep the promises they make to consumers about privacy and, in particular, the precautions they take to secure consumers' personal information. To respond to consumers' concerns about privacy, many Web sites post privacy policies that describe how consumers' personal information is collected, used, shared, and secured. Indeed, almost all the top 100 commercial sites now post privacy policies. Using its authority under Section 5 of the FTC Act, which prohibits unfair or deceptive practices, the Commission has brought a number of cases to enforce the promises in privacy statements, including promises about the security of consumers' personal information.

Early FTC Actions

The FTC has been enforcing Section 5 of the FTC Act at least as long ago as its GeoCities case in 1998. Other early FTC actions relating to on-line privacy include claims with Eli Lilly and Company (relating to sensitive information collected on its Prozac website); Microsoft Corp. (regarding the privacy and security of personal information collected from consumers through its "Passport" Web services); and Guess, Incorporated (relating to potential disclosure of credit card and other information).[20]

---

[19] http://www.ftc.gov/privacy/privacyinitiatives/promises.html.

[20] Details on all these cases are available at http://www.ftc.gov/opa.

FTC Settlements with TJX, Reed Elsevier (REI) and Seisint

In March 2008, the FTC announced a settlement with retailer TJX that it "failed to use reasonable and appropriate security measures to prevent unauthorized access to personal information on its computer networks." According to the FTC, an intruder

> exploited these failures and obtained tens of millions of credit and debit payment cards that consumers used at TJX's stores, as well as the personal information of approximately 455,000 consumers who returned merchandise to the stores. Banks have claimed that tens of millions of dollars in fraudulent charges have been made on the cards and millions of cards have been cancelled and reissued.

> Specifically, the agency charged that TJX:

> - Created an unnecessary risk to personal information by storing it on, and transmitting it between and within, its various computer networks in clear text;

> - Did not use readily available security measures to limit wireless access to its networks, thereby allowing an intruder to connect wirelessly to its networks without authorization;

> - Did not require network administrators and others to use strong passwords or to use different passwords to access different programs, computers, and networks;

> - Failed to use readily available security measures, such as firewalls, to limit access among its computers and the Internet; and

> - Failed to employ sufficient measures to detect and prevent unauthorized access to computer networks or to conduct security investigations, such as patching or updating anti-virus software.

In the same press release announcing the TJX settlement, the FTC announced similar settlements against data brokers Reed Elsevier (REI) and Seisint. The FTC complaint alleges that REI and Seisint systems contained numerous security failures that were exploited by identity thieves to obtain access to sensitive information about at least 316,000 consumers from Seisint databases. The identity thieves used the information to activate credit cards and open new accounts, and made fraudulent purchases on the cards and new accounts. The FTC explains:

> The settlement with TJX requires it to establish and maintain a comprehensive security program reasonably designed to protect the security, confidentiality, and integrity of personal information it collects from or about consumers. The settlement with REI and Seisint requires them to establish and maintain comprehensive security programs to protect personal information that is in whole or part nonpublic information. The settlements require the programs to contain administrative, technical, and physical safeguards appropriate to

each company's size, the nature of its activities, and the sensitivity of the personal information it collects. Specifically, the companies must:

- Designate an employee or employees to coordinate the information security program;

- Identify internal and external risks to the security and confidentiality of personal information and assess the safeguards already in place;

- Design and implement safeguards to control the risks identified in the risk assessment and monitor their effectiveness;

- Develop reasonable steps to select and oversee service providers that handle the personal information they receive from the companies; and

- Evaluate and adjust their information security programs to reflect the results of monitoring, any material changes to their operations, or other circumstances that may impact the effectiveness of their security programs;

The settlements require the companies to retain independent, third-party security auditors to assess their security programs on a biennial basis for the next 20 years. The auditors will be required to certify that the companies' security programs meet or exceed the requirements of the FTC's orders and are operating with sufficient effectiveness to provide reasonable assurance that the security of consumers' personal information is being protected.

In announcing these settlements, FTC Chairperson Deborah Platt Majoras said

By now, the message should be clear: companies that collect sensitive consumer information have a responsibility to keep it secure. These cases bring to 20 the number of complaints in which the FTC has charged companies with security deficiencies in protecting sensitive consumer information. Information security is a priority for the FTC, as it should be for every business in America.

CVS Caremark Settlement

In February 2009 CVS Caremark settled FTC charges that it failed to take reasonable and appropriate security measures to protect the sensitive financial and medical information of its customers and employees, in violation of federal law.[21] In a separate but related agreement, the company's pharmacy chain agreed to pay $2.25 million to resolve HHS allegations that it violated HIPAA.

In the FTC press release, William E. Kovacic, Chairman of the Federal Trade Commission, said

This is a case that will restore appropriate privacy protections to tens of millions of people across the country. … It also sends a strong message to other organizations that possess consumers' protected personal information. They are required to secure consumers' private information.

---

[21] Details are available at http://www.ftc.gov/opa.

Other FTC Settlements for Failing to Protect Sensitive Consumer Information

The FTC has conducted numerous enforcement against companies. Approximately 30 have resulted in a published settlement. Among them are the following:[22]

- BJ's Wholesale Club (retailer), 2005

- Life is Good (apparel retailer), 2008

- Goal Financial, LLC (student lender), 2008

- ChoicePoint (consumer data broker), 2006 and 2009

These FTC settlements show that companies that ignore their responsibility to secure their information assets will be held accountable.

3.4.8 **STATE BREACH DISCLOSURE AND RELATED ISS AND PRIVACY LAWS**

Further complicating the legal landscape are the numerous state laws regarding information security. Because there are 50 states, the volume of laws can be overwhelming.

On July 1, 2003, California Civil Code 1798.80-84 became the first state law requiring that consumers be notified in the event that an organization had reason to believe that it had suffered a computer breach in which personal information about California residents had been compromised.

At the time of this writing, 46 other states, plus the District of Columbia, Puerto Rico, and the Virgin Islands, have enacted legislation requiring notification of security breaches involving information.[23] Compliance must include all of these laws that apply to one's organization.

States have also been active in writing information security and data privacy protection laws (e.g., California Civil Code 1798.81.5). Massachusetts regulations (201 CMR 17.00) provide minimum standards for safeguarding personal information for any business that owns or sells personal data of Massachusetts residents. Companies possessing such data are required to develop and monitor a comprehensive written information security program, designate an employee to be responsible for the program, implement training, establish policies regarding access to the data, use encryption, and require that service providers comply with these requirements in all written contracts.

---

[22] Details are available at http://www.ftc.gov/opa.

[23] The National Conference of State Legislatures maintains a list of state security-breach notification laws, including hyperlinks to the various state laws, http://www.ncsl.org/IssuesResearch/TelecommunicationsInformationTechnology/SecurityBreach NotificationLaws/tabid/13489/Default.aspx.

Minnesota, Nevada, and Washington have passed legislation allowing banks to recover costs and damages from retailers and credit card processors that suffer data breaches after failing to comply with current Payment Card Industry (PCI) standards.

The landscape is bound to get more complicated. Intellectual property attorney Stephen Wu observes (2010):

> I expect states to continue testing the effectiveness of relatively modest and incremental legislation. Yet, with the huge cost of data breaches, small and large, it is more important than ever for businesses to adopt security programs from a risk management perspective, even if they have no legislative or regulatory requirement to do so.

3.4.9 EUROPEAN UNION DATA PROTECTION DIRECTIVE

In 1995, the European Commission issued the EU Data Protection Directive (Directive 95/46/EC). The directive is designed to harmonize the national laws of the EU member states that are aimed at protecting the privacy and protection of all personal data collected for or about citizens of the EU. The directive, which took effect in the fall of 1998, creates a standardized framework for on-line privacy rights, establishing minimum standards that the data protection legislation of each EU member nation must meet.

The directive is supplemented by Directive 2002/22/EC or ePrivacy Directive, which addresses the privacy of electronic communications and the use of cookies and clarifies the rules that apply to unsolicited commercial messages. That Directive has been amended by Directive 2009/136/EC, which requires the EU member states to modify their national laws accordingly by June 2011.

U.S.–EU Safe Harbor

The EU Data Protection Directive requires that member state national laws prohibit the transfer of personal data outside of the EU except when the recipient demonstrates it will provide an adequate level of protection for individual privacy consistent with the directive's standards.

To provide a streamlined means for U.S. organizations to comply with the directive and to take account of different approaches to privacy between the EU and the United States, the U.S. Department of Commerce in consultation with the European Commission developed a safe harbor framework through which a U.S. organization could demonstrate that it provides an adequate level of protection for personal information of EU citizens.

The U.S. Department of Commerce (2000) has documented seven key privacy principles that EU Directive 94/46/EC requires:

NOTICE: An organization must inform individuals about the purposes for which it collects and uses information about them, how to contact the organization with any inquiries or complaints, the types of third parties to which it discloses the information, and the choices and means the organization offers individuals for limiting its use and disclosure. ...

CHOICE: An organization must offer individuals the opportunity to choose (opt out) whether their personal information is (a) to be disclosed to a third party* or (b) to be used for a purpose that is incompatible with the purpose(s) for which it was originally collected or subsequently authorized by the individual. ...

ONWARD TRANSFER: To disclose information to a third party, organizations must apply the Notice and Choice Principles. ...

SECURITY: Organizations creating, maintaining, using or disseminating personal information must take reasonable precautions to protect it from loss, misuse and unauthorized access, disclosure, alteration and destruction.

DATA INTEGRITY: Consistent with the Principles, personal information must be relevant for the purposes for which it is to be used. ...

ACCESS: Individuals must have access to personal information about them that an organization holds and be able to correct, amend, or delete that information where it is inaccurate ...

ENFORCEMENT: Effective privacy protection must include mechanisms for assuring compliance with the Principles, recourse for individuals to whom the data relate affected by non-compliance with the Principles, and consequences for the organization when the Principles are not followed. ...

* It is not necessary to provide notice or choice when disclosure is made to a third party that is acting as an agent to perform task(s) on behalf of and under the instructions of the organization. The Onward Transfer Principle, on the other hand, does apply to such disclosures.

3.4.10 EMERGING CASE LAW

Responsibility for On-Line Bank Theft

It was only a matter of time before cybercriminals would discover that breaking into company computer systems might give them access to on-line bank credentials. That seems to have happened on a large scale in the third quarter of 2009 when cybercriminals stole more in on-line bank theft than traditional robbers stole from brick-and-mortar banks. Krebs (2010, "Cyber crooks") points out that in the third quarter of 2009 cybercriminals stole more than $25 million in on-line bank theft, while traditional bank robbers netted less than $9.5 million during the same time period.

Cybercriminals are able to launch "man-in-the-middle" and other sophisticated attacks against businesses by taking advantage of technical weaknesses in information systems coupled with social engineering attacks directed to key personnel. Cybercriminals also plant malicious software on a victim's PC to steal the company's on-line banking credentials, and then use those credentials to siphon money from the targeted accounts.

Because these attacks use legitimate on-line bank credentials, banks claim they are under no legal requirement to reimburse a business for its losses so long as the bank uses commercially reasonable security measures as set forth in the Uniform Commercial Code § 4A-202 (Authorized and Verified Payment Orders).

Several business victims have filed lawsuits against their banks in an attempt to recover their losses:

- In September 2009, an Illinois district court allowed a business to sue its bank on the grounds that it may have failed to sufficiently secure their account, after an unidentified hacker obtained a $26,500 loan on the account using the customers' user name and password (Zetter, 2009).

- In September 2009, a construction firm in Maine sued a local bank after cyber thieves stole more than a half million dollars from the company in a sophisticated online bank heist (Citadel Information Group, 2009, September 23).

- In December 2009, an electronics testing firm in Louisiana sued its bank, Capital One, alleging that the financial institution was negligent when it failed to stop hackers from transferring nearly $100,000 out of its account (Citadel Information Group, 2009, December 7).

- In March 2009, a real estate appraisal company in Hammond, Louisiana, lost more than $27,000 when four unauthorized automated clearinghouse (ACH) withdrawals were made from its accounts and sent to individuals around the United States. The company is suing its bank, also Capital One, to recover its losses (Krebs, 2010, "Victim").

In an unusual case, PlainsCapital bank in Lubbock, Texas, is suing its customer, Hillary Machinery Inc. PlainsCapital cited a letter from Hillary that demanded repayment for an on-line loss, alleging that the bank failed to employ commercially reasonable security measures. The lawsuit asks the U.S. District Court for the Eastern District of Texas to certify that PlainsCapital's security was in fact reasonable, and that it processed the wire transfers in good faith. In documents filed with the court, the bank alleges that the fraudulent transactions were initiated using the defendant's valid on-line banking credentials (Krebs, 2010, "Texas").

Class Action Suits

Not surprisingly, class action suits have been filed against companies which have lost sensitive consumer information.

A shareholder class action lawsuit filed against Heartland Payment Systems over its data breach was dismissed in December 2009. The lawsuit had been filed by shareholders who alleged that Heartland failed to adequately safeguard the compromised consumer data and did not notify consumers about the breach in a timely manner as required by law (Mills, 2009).

In a consumer class action lawsuit for the same data breach, Heartland Payment Systems agreed to pay a minimum of $1 million and up to a maximum of $2.4 million to class members who submit valid claims for losses as a result of the intrusion. The company will also be responsible for $1.5 million for the cost of notice to the settling class and $760,000 to cover legal fees (Heartland, 2009).

In another consumer class action lawsuit, in April 2010 the United States District Court for the Western District of Kentucky began alerting consumers who provided their personal information or made mortgage payments to Countrywide about a proposed settlement reached in a class action lawsuit about stolen personal and financial information (Court, 2010). The lawsuit claimed that a senior financial advisor formerly employed by Countrywide took confidential information from millions of consumer records and sold it to third parties. The lawsuit further alleged that Countrywide did not adequately protect confidential personal and financial information of its clients. Under the proposed settlement Countrywide is to provide credit monitoring and identity theft insurance these consumers; cash reimbursements up to $6.5 million to identity theft victims; and plaintiff attorney fees of $3.625 million.

Obviously, as information systems become ubiquitous, the landscape in legal issues is still emerging. As Françoise Gilbert states in her discussion of information security and privacy issues (2008):

> There was a time, not so long ago, when the Internet was a world apart. We distinguished e-commerce and other activities in "cyberspace" from those that had existed for centuries in what we called the "brick and mortar" world. This is no longer the case. These worlds have converged.

Clearly there is increased accountability for information security, a complicated legislative landscape, and a rapidly changing legal landscape. Legal counsel should be involved not only during the development of an organization's ISS program but periodically afterwards to make sure the program complies with evolving laws and other legal obligations.

3.5 SPECIAL TOPICS IN ISS

This section examines three additional topics:

1. ISS risk and vulnerability assessment

2. policy implementation

3. incident response

After this examination, the reader will have been exposed to all the pieces of information systems security management (ISMS). The following section uses those pieces to build a comprehensive ISMS framework as required by ISO 27001.

3.5.1 ISS RISK AND VULNERABILITY ASSESSMENT

Every professional and legal standard described herein requires that an organization manage ISS using a risk-based approach.

A risk and vulnerability assessment is often conducted to measure compliance against a specific standard. For example, the Payment Card Industry Data Security Standard requires companies that take credit or debit cards to conduct an assessment against the current PCI DSS. A company seeking to be certified compliant with ISO 27001 will conduct a risk and vulnerability assessment in accordance with ISO 27001 standards. A third party receiving patient information from a medical center will need to assess its ability to meet HIPAA privacy requirements.

An ISS assessment generally addresses the traditional ISS objectives: protecting information systems; detecting system attacks, both successful and blocked; recovering from attacks; and complying with laws, regulations, and contractual obligations—while ensuring the confidentiality, integrity, and availability of the organization's data.

An ISS risk and vulnerability assessment generally has both management and technical components. The management component can range from very formal to very informal. At its most formal, the management component can have the rigor of a formal audit undertaken to demonstrate compliance with a documented standard. At its most informal, the management component may consist of structured interviews with selective management and staff, together with a review of available documentation. The technical component of the risk assessment provides the organization with a formal snapshot-in-time of the security of its IT infrastructure.

Regardless of how specific or general, how formal or informal, an ISS risk and vulnerability assessment can answer the following questions:

- What are the organization's information security needs, obligations, and opportunities?
    - legal obligations to protect information
    - ethical obligations to protect information of customers, trading partners, and others
    - brand risk from security incident
    - fiduciary responsibilities
    - competitive opportunities

- How effective is the organization at managing the security of its critical information assets?
    - administrative, technical, and physical controls
    - management structure
    - ISS policies
    - information classification and control
    - user awareness training and education
    - computer and network security
    - physical security
    - personnel security
    - third-party ISS assurance

- What are the gaps between its needs and its realities?
    - management gaps
    - technology gaps
    - cultural gaps

- What capacity exists for closing the gap?
    - time and resources
    - attention span
    - culture

Armed with this information, the organization may now make plans to methodically close its ISS gaps.

3.5.2 ISS POLICY IMPLEMENTATION

According to ISO 27002, information security policies should include, at a minimum, the following guidance:

- a definition of information security, its overall objectives and scope, and the importance of security as an enabling mechanism for information sharing

- a statement of management intent, supporting the goals and principles of information security

- a brief explanation of the security policies, principles, standards, and compliance requirements of particular importance to the organization

Management's biggest challenge lies not in the writing of specific policies but in the orderly development and implementation of policies. An organization can increase the odds that its information security policies will actually influence security by doing the following. Moreover, following a rigorous methodology for developing ISS policies prepares an organization for implementing an information security management system.

This eight-step process illustrates one methodology:

Step 1   Identify organizational issues that impact ISS policy.

Step 2   Identify the information in need of protection and the protection required.

Step 3   Identify the various classes of policy users.

Step 4   Draft ISS policies based on Steps 1–3.

Step 5   Review draft policies with management, users, and legal counsel, and then finalize.

Step 6   Train all personnel in the organization's ISS policies.

Step 7   Enforce the ISS policies.

Step 8   Review and modify policies, as appropriate but at least annually.

3.5.3 INCIDENT RESPONSE

Information security incident response is a critical skill set for the inevitable problems related to information security. Such problems include all the types of incidents already described, including malware, hacking, and errors. According to NIST (Scarfone, K., Grance, T., & Masone, K., 2008, p. ES-1):

> Computer security incident response has become an important component of information technology (IT) programs. Security-related threats have become not only more numerous and diverse but also more damaging and disruptive. New types of security-related incidents emerge frequently. Preventative activities based on the results of risk assessments can lower the number of incidents, but not all incidents can be prevented. An incident response capability is therefore necessary for rapidly detecting incidents, minimizing loss and destruction, mitigating the weaknesses that were exploited, and restoring computing services.

According to CERT, a well-known information security response unit of Carnegie Mellon University, there are 19 steps to developing a computer security incident response team (CSIRT) (CERT, 2006):

1. Identify stakeholders and participants.
2. Obtain management support and sponsorship.
3. Develop a CSIRT project plan.
4. Gather information.
5. Identify the CSIRT constituency.
6. Define the CSIRT mission.
7. Secure funding for CSIRT operations.
8. Decide on the range and level of services the CSIRT will offer.
9. Determine the CSIRT reporting structure, authority and organizational model.
10. Identify required resources such as staff, equipment and infrastructure.
11. Define interactions and interfaces.
12. Define roles, responsibilities and the corresponding authority.
13. Document the workflow.
14. Develop policies and corresponding procedures.
15. Create an implementation plan and solicit feedback.
16. Announce the CSIRT when it becomes operational.
17. Define methods for evaluating the performance of the CSIRT.
18. Have a backup plan for every element of the CSIRT.
19. Be flexible.

The creation of an incident response team is also discussed by SANS, a noted information security authority (using a different name for the team):

> No company's security policy should be considered complete until procedures are put into place that allow for the handling and recovery from even the most devastating of incidents. One possible solution is the inclusion a Computer Incident Response Team (CIRT) within the company's incident response procedures.

NIST, CERT, and SANS have many helpful documents for developing information security incident response plans. One of the most critical elements of the plan is the policy document. NIST defines the policy elements of incident response to be (Scarfone, K., Grance, T., & Masone, K., 2008, p. 2-3):

- Statement of management commitment

- Purpose and objectives of the policy

- Scope of the policy (to whom and what it applies and under what circumstances)

- Definition of computer security incidents and their consequences within the context of the organization

- Organizational structure and delineation of roles, responsibilities, and levels of authority; should include the authority of the incident response team to confiscate or disconnect equipment and to monitor suspicious activity, and the requirements for reporting certain types of incidents

- Prioritization or severity ratings of incidents

- Performance measures

- Reporting and contact forms

The CSIRT or CIRT forms the essential response capability to remediate an incident. Physical security can be a critical element of this team, especially because of the similarities in incident response between physical and information security paradigms. As the physical security practitioner well knows, being prepared to respond to incidents is a critical aspect of any security program.

3.6   **TOTAL ISS MANAGEMENT**

Risks, threats, vulnerabilities, and countermeasures are all evolving. As cybercriminals get better at their craft, defenders must get better at theirs. Likewise, the better the bad guys are, the more likely laws, regulations, and contracts will be strengthened to require improved information systems security. The resulting arms race gives rise to what's known as the Red Queen Effect.[24]

In a broad sense, consistent with other evolving management best practices, the Red Queen Effect requires that an organization's information systems management program must be continually improved.

This means that the function of management cannot just be to provide an appropriate level of information systems security today. ISS management must also accept the responsibility of doing a better job tomorrow. That is the purpose of the information security management system (ISMS).

3.6.1   **ISO 27001 INFORMATION SECURITY MANAGEMENT SYSTEMS**

The centerpiece of ISO 27001 is the ISMS, the keystone for continual improvement in the organization's ability to effectively manage the security of its information assets.

An organization's ISMS is that part of the organization's (ISO 27001, p. 2)

> overall management system, based on a business risk approach, to establish, implement, operate, monitor, review and improve information security. ... The management system includes organizational structure, policies, planning activities, responsibilities, practices, procedures, processes and resources.

An ISMS is based upon a process-model perspective of information security management (ISO 27001, p. v):

> The process approach for information security management presented in this International Standard encourages its users to emphasize the importance of:
>
> a) **understanding** an organization's information security requirements and the need to establish policy and objectives for information security;
>
> b) **implementing** operating controls to manage an organization's information security risks in the context of the organization's overall business risk;

---

[24] The phrase comes from Lewis Carroll's *Through the Looking Glass*, in which the Red Queen says to Alice, "Now, *here*, you see, it takes all the running you can do, to keep in the same place."

   c) **monitoring** and reviewing the performance and effectiveness of the ISMS; and

   d) **continual improvement** based on objective measurement.

The following diagram based on ISO 27001 illustrates the spiral-based plan-do-check-act (PDCA) model.

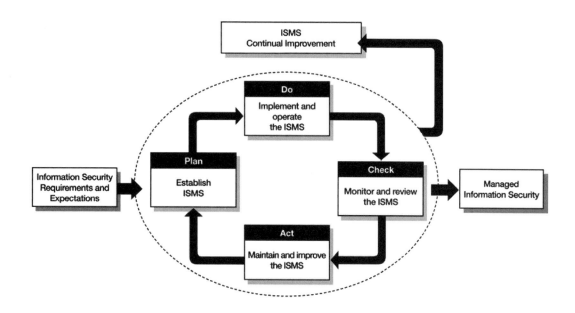

Figure 3-15
Plan-Do-Check-Act Model Applied to ISMS Processes

On the left, as continual input to the PDCA model, are evolving information security requirements and expectations. On the right, as continual output from the PDCA model, is an ever-improving capacity to manage the security needs of the organization. An ISMS based on the continuous progression of plan-do-check-act can generate continual improvement.

ISO 27001 defines the four PDCA phases as follows:

Plan	**Establish the ISMS.**	

Plan **Establish the ISMS.**
Establish ISMS policy, objectives, processes, and procedures relevant to managing risk and improving information security in alignment with an organization's overall policies and objectives.

Do **Implement and Operate the ISMS.**
Implement and operate the ISMS policy, controls, processes, and procedures.

Check **Monitor and Review the ISMS.**
Assess and as applicable measure process performance against ISMS policy, objectives, and practical experience; reporting the results to management for review

Act **Maintain and Improve the ISMS.**
Continually improve the ISMS by taking corrective and preventive actions based on the results of internal ISMS audits, management reviews, and other relevant information.

3.6.2 MAKING CONTINUAL IMPROVEMENT HAPPEN

The fundamental idea behind an ISMS is continual improvement, always getting better, always raising the bar. Many continual improvement programs have been developed, implemented, and tested over the last 40 years. Much has been learned about what works and what does not when implementing such programs. Certainly one key factor is organizational culture.[25]

---

[25] See, e.g., the following: W. E. Deming on continuous improvement (*The New Economics*, 1994); Peter Senge's equally seminal book on learning organizations, (*The Fifth Discipline*, 1990); Stan Stahl's explication of Barry Boehm's Theory-W, ("User Involvement in Project Success" in H. Tipton & M. Krause, *Information Security Management Handbook*, 1997); and Tom Petzinger's insightful stories of what actually works on the front lines, (*The New Pioneers*, 1999).

An ISS-Aware Culture

The effectiveness of an information security program ultimately depends upon people's behavior.[26] Behavior, in turn, depends on what people know, how they feel, and what their instincts tell them to do. While an ISS awareness training program can impart information security knowledge, it rarely has significant impact on people's deeper security instincts. The result is often a gap between the dictates of information security policy and the behaviors of people. Unless people's feeling and instincts about information security change, the gap will persist. It is the role of culture to close that gap.

The culture of an organization can be defined as follows (Schein, 1992):

> A pattern of shared basic assumptions that the group learned as it solved its problems of external adaptation and internal integration, that has worked well enough to be considered valid and, therefore, to be taught to new members as the correct way to perceive, think, and feel in relation to those problems.

As an organization evolves, it discovers ways to adapt to market, competitive, regulatory, and other changes in its external environment. It also figures out ways to organize itself internally —both formally (according to the organization chart) and informally (the way the work actually gets done). These ways become the norm for the organization; they become its culture.

ISS Cultural Challenge

Several cultural realities affect the organization's ability to secure its information systems and the sensitive information they contains:

- **ISS is a new kid on the block.** In most organizations the ISS function has not been in existence as long as other departments. The field itself dates only to 1970.[27]

- **ISS is nowhere near core to the organization.** Even when there is a regulatory requirement for information security controls, these are pushed by senior management only because they are legally required. Top-level support for ISS could dry up in an instant if the legal and regulatory landscape were to change.

---

[26] This section is based on S. Stahl, "Beyond Information Security Awareness Training: It's Time to Change the Culture," in H. Tipton and M. Krause (Eds.), *Information Security Management Handbook* (3rd ed.), Boca Raton, FL: Auerbach Publications, 2006.

[27] The origin of the field can be set as the publication date of *Security Controls for Computer Systems, Report of Defense Science Board Task Force on Computer Security*, edited by W. Ware. A classified version was published in 1970 for the Office of the Secretary of Defense. The Rand Corporation published an unclassified version in 1979.

- **ISS concerns seem disconnected from those of the marketing, sales, operations, and financial organizations.** As a result, the ISS subculture finds itself subordinate to the other, more dominant subcultures.

- **"Information systems security" contains the word "security."** The cultural expectation is that the ISS group will, like other security functions, take care of its own issues without requiring other employees to get involved.

- **ISS Security culture touches the rest of the organization mainly when someone forgets his password or when the system prevents someone from doing his job.** Except for the annual awareness training, there are few natural opportunities for cultural blending, leading the ISS subculture to evolve in isolation from the dominant culture.

It is against this backdrop that the information security organization must embed its culture into the culture of the larger organization. That is the only way to transfer to the larger organization the correct way to perceive, think, and feel in relation to ISS challenges. Schein (p. 15) observes:

> Culture and leadership are two sides of the same coin … If cultures become dysfunctional, it is the unique function of leadership to perceive the functional and dysfunctional elements of the existing culture and to manage cultural evolution and change in such a way that the group can survive in a changing environment.
>
> Leadership … is the ability to step outside the culture … and to start evolutionary change processes that are … adaptive. This ability to perceive the limitations of one's own culture and to develop the culture adaptively is the essence and ultimate challenge of leadership.

This aspect of leadership—to change the larger culture in the direction of information security—is a critical role for security practitioners. Until the information security way of seeing the world becomes a part of the organization's culture, the organization is dysfunctional. Every time there is a security breach whose root cause is human provides evidence of the dysfunction.

ISS has become forever intertwined with the practice of the physical security practitioner. Security practitioners should examine their organization's culture from the outside, molding and shaping its evolution, so that over time employees do the right thing: they are careful, they pay attention, and they even train each other–all because an information security mindset has become embedded in the larger culture.

APPENDIX A

INFORMATION SYSTEMS SECURITY RESOURCES

ISS-Related Organizations

ASIS International. ASIS provides numerous ISS-related resources, including member networking; the Information Resources Center; *Security Management* magazine, along with daily and weekly on-line editions; and the Information Technology Security Council. http://www.asisonline.org

Center for Internet Security (CIS). CIS is a leader in information security metrics and provides hardening guides for ensuring systems are properly configured. It provides both free and fee-based services. http://cisecurity.org

Community Emergency Response Team (CERT). This program from Carnegie Mellon University provides a wide range of resources for addressing information security issues. http://www.cert.org

Computer Security Institute (CSI). CSI is perhaps best known for its two annual conferences and its annual computer crime and security survey, published in conjunction with the FBI. http://www.gocsi.com

Information Systems Audit and Control Association (ISAC). This organization, which focuses on audit and controls, has 86,000 members spread across 160 chapters worldwide. http://isaca.org

Information Systems Security Association (ISSA). ISSA, the preeminent organization for information security professionals, is an international, not-for-profit organization that promotes education and advocacy. ISSA has 142 chapters and 10,000 members in 70 countries worldwide. https://www.issa.org

InfraGard. This FBI/private sector collaboration provides numerous information security resources. http://www.infragard.net

The National Institute of Standards and Technology (NIST). NIST is a non-regulatory federal agency of the US government within the U.S. Department of Commerce. Its mission is to promote U.S. innovation and industrial competitiveness by advancing measurement science, standards, and technology. NIST offers much guidance on information security, and its Web site lists many information security professional organizations. http://www.nist.gov

Open Web Application Security Project (OWASP). This is a resource regarding Web application security issues. http://www.owasp.org

Privacy Rights Clearinghouse (PRC). This nonprofit provides consumer information and consumer advocacy and is a source for breach-disclosure data. http://www.privacyrights.org

Secunia. This is a useful resource for patches and vulnerabilities. http://secunia.com

System Administration, Networking, and Security Institute (SANS). This is one of the preeminent training and knowledge repositories in the information security industry. It provides reputable training programs and also runs the Internet Storm Center (http://isc.sans.org), which is known for its daily updates by volunteer incident handlers. http://www.sans.org

Information Security Certifications

Certified Information Security Manager (CISM) and Certified Information Security Auditor (CISA). These certifications come from ISACA. http://www.isaca.org

Certified Information Systems Security Practitioner (CISSP). This certification from the International Information Systems Security Certification Consortium is considered the gold standard. https://www.isc2.org

Global Information Assurance Certification (GIAC). This certification is available in several ISS specialties. http://www.giac.org

A list of ISS certifications can found at https://www.issa.org.

Information Systems Security Advisories and Technical Blogs

CERT Coordination Center/Carnegie Mellon University. http://www.cert.org/

Google Online Security Blog. http://googleonlinesecurity.blogspot.com/

Microsoft Malware Protection Center: Threat Research & Response Blog. http://blogs.technet.com/mmpc/default.aspx

SANS Internet Storm Center. http://isc.sans.org

US CERT. http://www.uscert.gov

ISS Non-Technical Blogs

CitadelOnSecurity. CitadelOnSecurity provides news and perspective on the world of cybercrime. Categories include business at risk, laws and regulations, financial systems security, social networks, national security, and vulnerability management. http://blog.citadel-information.com

KrebsOnSecurity. Brian Krebs is a former *Washington Post* reporter whose beat included cybercrime. The blog features posts on a number of recurring themes, including on-line crime investigations, the latest threats, security updates, data breaches, and occasionally cyber justice. http://www.krebsonsecurity.com/

Schneier on Security. Bruce Schneier is an internationally renowned security technologist and author, described by *The Economist* as a security guru. http://www.schneier.com

Emerging Legal Framework

United States Federal Laws & Regulations
Federal Trade Commission, Standards for Safeguarding Customer Information, 16 CFR 314

Health Insurance Portability and Accountability Act, 45 CFR 160 & 164

Privacy and Consumer Financial Information, 12 CFR 40

Sarbanes-Oxley Act of 2002, Public Law 107-204, Section 404

California Civil Code
Breach Disclosure Law, California Civil Code 1798.80-84

California Office of Privacy Protection. (2008). *California business privacy handbook.* http://www.privacy. ca.gov/ business/ca_business_privacy_hb.pdf

Other Legal References
Braun, R., & Stahl, S. (2005). An emerging information security minimum standard of due care. In H. Tipton and M. Krause (Eds.), *Information security management handbook* (6th ed.). Boca Raton, FL: Auerbach Publications.

Braun, R., & Stahl, S. (2006, March). An emerging information security minimum standard of due care, *Privacy and Data Security Law Journal.*

Cook, W. (2004, June). Open (trade) secrets: CSO Online. Available: http://www.csoonline.com/ article/219313/open-trade-secrets [2010, December 5].

Information Security Governance

Business Roundtable. (2004). Securing cyberspace: Business roundtable's framework for the future. Available: http://citadel-information.com/library/2/securing-cyberspace-business-roundtables-framework-for-future-040520.pdf [2010, December 5].

ISACA. (2001). Information security governance: Guidance for boards of directors and executive management, 2nd ed. Rolling Meadows, IL: ISACA, 2001.

National Cyber Security Summit Task Force. (2004). Corporate Governance Task Force report: Information security governance: A call to action. National Cyber Security Partnership. Available: http://citadel-information.com/library/2/infosec-governance-national-cybersecurity-partnership-040412.pdf [2010, December 5].

ISS Management Guides, Standards, and Practices

Information technology—security techniques—code of practice for information security management, ISO 17799. (2000). Geneva: International Organization for Standardization.

PCI Security Standards Council. (2010). *Payment card industry (PCI) data security standard.* Available: https://www.pcisecuritystandards.org/documents/pci_dss_v2.pdf [2010, December 5].

National Institute of Standards & Technology publications:

> Bowen, P., Hash, J. & Wilson, M. (2006). *Information security handbook: A guide for managers.* Special Publication 800-100. Gaithersburg, MD: NIST.

> Grance, T., Hash, J., Peck, S., Smith, J., & Korow-Diks, K. (2002). *Security guide for interconnecting information technology systems.* Special Publication 800-47. Gaithersburg, MD: NIST.

> Kent, K., Chevalier, S., Grance, T., & Dang, H. (2006). *Guide to integrating forensic techniques into incident response.* Special Publication 800-86. Gaithersburg, MD: NIST.

> Kent, K., & Souppaya, M. (2006). *Guide to computer security log management.* Special Publication 800-92. Gaithersburg, MD: NIST.

> Kissel, R., Stine, K., Scholl, M., Rossman, H., Fahlsing, J., & Gulick, J. (2008). *Security considerations in the information system development life cycle.* Special Publication 800-64. Gaithersburg, MD: NIST.

> Kuhn, D., Walsh, T., & Fries, S. (2005). *Security considerations for voice over IP systems.* Special Publication 800-58. Gaithersburg, MD: NIST.

Mell, P., Kent, K., & Nusbaum, J. (2005). *Guide to malware incident prevention and handling.* Special Publication 800-83. Gaithersburg, MD: NIST.

Scarfone, K., Grance, T., & Masone, K. (2008). *Computer security incident handling guide,* Special Publication 800-61. Gaithersburg, MD: NIST.

Scarfone, K., & Mell, P. (2007). *Guide to intrusion detection and prevention (IDP) systems.* Special Publication 800-94. Gaithersburg, MD: NIST.

Wilson, M., & Hash, J. (2003). *Building an information technology security awareness and training program.* Special Publication 800-50. Gaithersburg, MD: NIST.

Specification for information security management system. In ISO 27001. (2005). Information technology—security techniques—information security management systems—requirements. Geneva: International Organization for Standardization.

Technology Configuration Guides

Microsoft Corporation. (2009). *Windows Server 2003 security guide.* Available: http://www.microsoft.com/downloads/en/details.aspx?FamilyID=8A2643C1-0685-4D89-B655-521EA6C7B4DB [2010, December 5]

National Security Agency. Multiple guides available. http://www.nsa.gov

Information Systems Crime and Security Surveys

Annual CSI Computer Crime and Security Survey. http://gocsi.com

REFERENCES

Borodkin, M. (2001). Computer incident response team. SANS Institute. Available: http://www.sans.org/reading_room/whitepapers/incident/computer-incident-response-team_641 [2010, December 5].

CERT. (2006). Action list for developing a computer security incident response team (CSIRT). Available: http://www.cert.org/csirts/action_list.html [2010, December 5].

Citadel Information Group. (2009, September 23). Company sues bank after $588,000 stolen by cyberthieves. Citadel on Security. Available: http://citadelonsecurity.blogspot.com/2009/09/another-corporate-victim-of-cybertheft.html [2010, December 5].

Citadel Information Group. (2009, December 7). La. firm sues Capital One after losing thousands in online bank fraud. Citadel on Security. Available: http://citadelonsecurity.blogspot.com/2009/12/la-firm-sues-capital-one-after-losing.html [2010, December 5].

Cordeiro, B. (2010, January 8). UPDATE 2-Heartland in $60 mln settlement with Visa, shares rise. Reuters. http://www.reuters.com/article/idUSSGE607019920100108.

Court to notify Countrywide customers about a class action settlement involving the theft of personal and financial data. (2010, April 12). PR Newswire. Available: http://www.prnewswire.com/news-releases/court-to-notify-countrywide-customers-about-a-class-action-settlement-involving-the-theft-of-personal-and-financial-data-90601539.html [2010, December 5].

Gilbert, F. (2008, February). Hot issues in cyberspace: Critical information privacy and security issues. *The Practical Lawyer*. Available: http://www.itlawgroup.com/resources/articles/139-marketing-and-sales.html [2010, December 5].

Gregg, M. (2009). *CISSP exam cram*. New York, NY: Pearson Publishing.

Heartland to pay up to $2.4 million to settle cardholder class action suit. (2009, December 21). DataBreaches.net. Available: http://www.databreaches.net/?p=8991 [2010, December 5].

ISACA. (2001). Information Security *Governance: Guidance for Boards of Directors and Executive Management,* 2nd ed. Rolling Meadows, IL: ISACA, 2001.

ISO 27001. (2005). Information technology—security techniques—information security management systems—requirements.

ISO 27002. (2005). Information technology—security techniques—code of practice for information security management.

Krebs, B. (2010). Cyber crooks leave traditional bank robbers in the dust. Krebs on Security. Available: http://krebsonsecurity.com/2010/03/cyber-crooks-leave-bank-robbers-in-the-dust [2010, December 5].

Krebs, B. (2010). Texas bank sues customer hit by $800,000 cyber heist. Krebs on Security. Available: http://krebsonsecurity.com/2010/01/texas-bank-sues-customer-hit-by-800000-cyber-heist [2010, December 5].

Krebs, B. (2010). Victim asks Capital One, 'Who's in your wallet?' Krebs on Security. Available: http://krebsonsecurity.com/2010/03/another-la-e-banking-victim-suing-capital-one/#more-700 [2010, December 5].

Kurzweil, R., *The Age of Spiritual Machines*, Viking Penguin, 1999.

Lam, D., Pease, K., Stahl, S., & Takamine, K. (2007, July). Creating the information security village. *ISSA Journal.*

Mills, E. (2009, December 10). Heartland data breach lawsuit dismissed. CNET News. Available: http://news.cnet.com/8301-1009_3-10413194-83.html [2010, December 5].

O'Brien, K. (2009, December 28). Cellphone encryption code is divulged. *New York Times.*

Organisation for Economic Co-operation and Development. (2002). *OECD guidelines for the security of information systems and networks—Towards a culture of security.* Paris: OECD. Available: http://www.oecd.org/dataoecd/16/ 22/15582260.pdf [2010, December 5].

PCI Security Standards Council. (2010). *Payment card industry (PCI) data security standard.* Available: https://www.pcisecuritystandards.org/documents/pci_dss_v2.pdf [2010, December 5].

Quigley, F., & Stahl, S. (1987). *Fundamental elements of information security.* TRW internal report.

Reed, D. (2003). Applying the OSI Seven Layer Network Model to information security. NIST. Available: http://www.isd.mel.nist.gov/projects/processcontrol/members/minutes/7-Sep-2004/OSI.pdf [2010, December 5].

SANS. (2006). Extranet policy. Available: http://www.sans.org/security-resources/policies/Extranet_Policy.doc [2010, December 5].

Scarfone, K., Grance, T., & Masone, K. (2008). *Computer security incident handling guide.* Gaithersburg, MD: National Institute of Standards and Technology.

Schein, E. (1992). *Organizational culture and leadership* (2nd ed.). San Francisco, CA: Jossey-Bass.

Stahl, S. (2006). Beyond information security awareness training: It's time to change the culture. In H. Tipton and M. Krause (Eds.), *Information Security Management Handbook* (3rd ed.). Boca Raton, FL: Auerbach Publications.

Turing, A. (1936-7). On computable numbers, with an application to the *Entscheidungsproblem*. *Proceedings of the London Mathematical Society*, Ser 2, vol. 42, pp. 230-265; corrections, ibid, vol 43, pp. 544-46.

U.S. Department of Commerce. (2000). Safe harbor privacy principals. Available: http://www. export.gov/safeharbor/eg_main_018247.asp [2010, December 6].

Wright, R. (2000). *Nonzero: the logic of human destiny*. New York, NY: Vintage.

Wu, S. (2010). Trends in state security and privacy laws and regulations. In *Privacy and Data Security Law Institute*. New York, NY: Practising Law Institute.

Zetter, K. (2009, September 4). Court Allows Woman to Sue Bank for Lax Security After $26,000 Stolen by Hacker. Wired (on-line). Available: http://www.wired.com/threatlevel/2009/09/citizens-financial-sued [2010, December 5].

CHAPTER 4
SECURITY CHALLENGES OF CONVERGENCE

By one definition, convergence is (Tyson, 2007, p. 4)

> the integration, in a formal, collaborative, and strategic manner, of the cumulative security resources of the organization in order to deliver enterprise-wide benefits through enhanced risk mitigation, increased operational effectiveness and efficiency, and cost savings.

Security convergence can indeed enhance risk mitigation, but it can also increase total organizational risk. This section examines the security challenges of convergence by first presenting two common examples (camera and access control systems). It then describes how a comprehensive information security management system (ISMS) can be the "formal, collaborative, and strategic" element required to mitigate risk.

4.1 NETWORK RISK

When physical security practitioners put physical security technology onto the network, they open the door to significant network-based security risk. For example, all of the following matters of interest to the information systems security (ISS) practitioner can also weaken physical security:

- **Denial of services (DOS):** the ability of a malicious individual to stop the functioning of a computer-based system

- **Insertion of inaccurate data:** adding incorrect data into a database or file

- **Data theft:** stealing data from a system

- **Data modification:** changing data or information on a system

- **Data destruction:** destroying data on a system

ISS principles center on three basic elements: confidentiality, integrity, and availability, also called the CIA triad. Those principles apply to the preceding issues as follows:

- **Denial of services (DOS):** availability
- **Insertion of inaccurate data:** integrity
- **Data theft:** confidentiality
- **Data modification:** integrity
- **Data destruction:** availability

To address the security risks brought on by convergence, physical security practitioners must be able to categorize ISS risk according to the CIA triad. This approach helps one quickly assess the types of risks faced and then apply the right strategies to mitigate those risk.

4.1.1 NETWORK CASE STUDY: CAMERA SYSTEM

A modern video surveillance system relies heavily on networks, as Figure 4-1 illustrates.

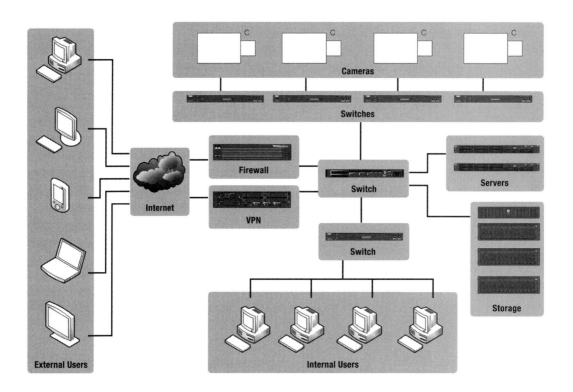

Figure 4-1
Networked Video System

The left side of Figure 4-1 shows external users on the Internet who could potentially connect to an organization's internal systems. Those users are segregated from the internal network by a firewall and a virtual private network (VPN) device. At the bottom of the diagram are internal users, who typically reach data assets via a network switch, the device that connects network assets together. At the top of the diagram are video cameras, which are typically dispersed throughout a company. Each camera connects to a switch, allowing each camera to talk to other devices on the network. Some switches connect to other switches so all of the devices can talk to each other.

The right side of the diagram shows the servers that control the video cameras. One server records the video while another provides command and control for the entire set of physical security systems. Beneath these two servers is a storage area network, on which all of the data resides.

The five risk issues named earlier could apply to the networked video system in Figure 4-1 as follows:

- **Denial of services (DOS).** Video cameras can have their video blocked from reaching client workstations and recording devices. Individuals bent on gaining unauthorized access to the facility might turn off video viewing capability.

- **Insertion of inaccurate data.** Inaccurate data can be inserted for recorded video, perhaps adding an invalid video between valid video streams. Someone who stole something from the facility might insert a video during that time that showed no one there.

- **Data theft.** Video streams could be stolen and used with bad intentions. Bank robbers, for example, might be able to analyze camera feeds to help them plan a bank robbery.

- **Data modification.** Data could modified while the video was in transit, by intercepting the correct video and showing previously recorded video to the operator, perhaps while perpetrating a crime.

- **Data destruction.** Video evidence recorded on a hard drive could be deleted, hiding evidence of a theft.

Each device in the diagram is communicating on the network and is potentially capable of communicating with everything else on the network. The users on the internal network are capable of talking to the servers and capable of talking to the video cameras. Someone who can talk to a network-enabled device may be able to control the physical security element or elements connected to it, possibly from anywhere in the world.

4.1.2 **NETWORK CASE STUDY: ACCESS CONTROL**

An electronic access control system raises additional nuances important to physical security practitioners. Figure 4-2 depicts a system layout.

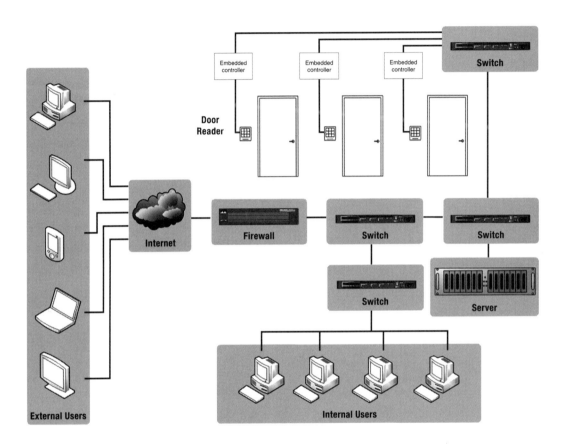

Figure 4-2
Networked Access Control System

The network architecture is similar to that of the video system (Figure 4-1). In Figure 4-2, internal users are shown at the bottom while external users are on the left. External users are segregated from internal users by a security device, in this case a firewall. All the elements on the network are connected via switches, including the access control server, the users, and the embedded controller. The door reader, also referred to as a card reader, is connected to the embedded controller, which is connected to the network.

The access control card reader talks directly to an embedded device that talks to the network. The embedded controller decides whether someone may enter through that door.

The card reader talks to the embedded controller which talks to the network.

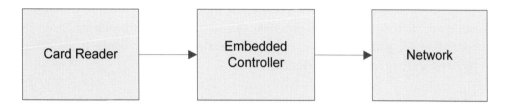

Figure 4-3
Access Control System Communication:
Reader to Controller to Network

Alternatively, a server speaks directly to the network. It does not need an intermediary.

Figure 4-4
Access Control System Communication:
Server to Network

The access control devices in Figure 4-2 are either connected directly to the network or connected to a device that can control them, which is connected to the network.

Computers communicate directly and indirectly. Computers communicate directly (also called layer 2) when they can see each other and indirectly (also called layer 3) when they need an intermediary. Direct communication is like speaking to someone else in a conference room. If John wants to talk to Mary in that conference room, he says, "Mary, can I talk to you?" When Mary acknowledges John, they have a conversation. If John needed to talk to someone outside the conference room, he would need an intermediary—a phone that knows how to dial the other person's phone and enable the conversation.

Direct communication between computers, that is layer 2 communication, occurs in the same way. The workstation that wants to talk to the access control server says, "Is the access control server available for me to talk to directly?" In other words, is the computer in the room? If so, they have a conversation.

Figure 4-5 shows the logical communication flow that takes place during a conversation between a workstation and the server that manages all the access control information.

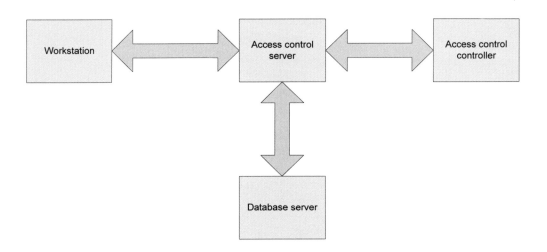

Figure 4-5
Logical Communication Flow

The workstation, left, talks to the access control server. The access control server takes whatever request the workstation makes (say to activate a card), communicates the request to the database server, and when the database server responds, the access control server sends a communication back to the workstation. All of this occurs in individual conversations between two computers, one after the other.

For this conversation to happen directly, all the machines must be on the same switch and therefore able to see each other. Figure 4-6 shows the access control elements connected to a switch.

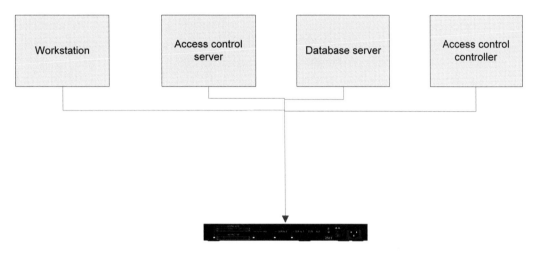

Figure 4-6
Access Control Elements Connected to Switch

In Figure 4-6, for the workstation to communicate to the access control server, it needs to send a signal to the switch, which then sends a copy of that signal to the access control server. Typically, the switch would not send the same signal to the database server, because it is not intended for the database server. Figure 4-7 shows how such communication occurs at layer 2:

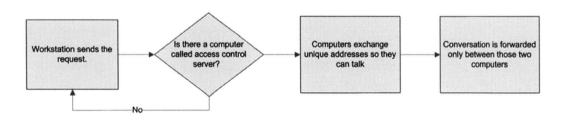

Figure 4-7
Layer 2 Communication

First, the workstation sends the request to talk to the access control server. If the access control server can be seen by the workstation, it sends back a unique address in the form of an acknowledgment so the workstation can communicate with it.

Returning to the conference room example may help explain the next level of computer communication. If John cannot see Mary, he knows Mary is not in the room. So, he picks up the phone and calls her. The phone is an intermediary facilitating communication. John and Mary are in different rooms, different cities, or different countries. In the computer example, if two computers cannot see each other directly, they are on separate networks and must use a router as an intermediary to communicate with each other.

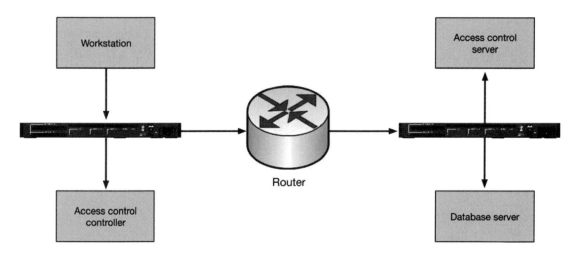

Figure 4-8
Access Control Router Communication

As Figure 4-8 shows, if the workstation wants to talk to the access control controller, it can just do so because the workstation can see the access control controller. It is on the same switch (analogous to being in the same conference room). To communicate with the access control server, however, the workstation first starts off by seeing whether the access control server is on the same network. If not, it asks the router whether it can get to the access control server. If the router can redirect it, it does so.

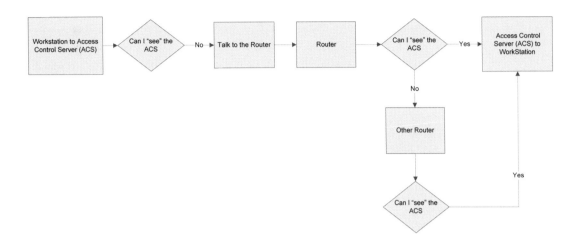

Figure 4-9
Workstation to Access Control Server Data Flow

Layer 3 communication is the mechanism that allows for computers to interact across the Internet around the world. There is little difference between the diagram in Figure 4-9 and what happens every day on the Internet. In a converged paradigm, an organization's computers and physical security assets are potentially accessible from across the world—and are therefore vulnerable.

These communications rules apply to every element which operates on the network. Every device connected to the network is accessible to everything else connected to the network.

The five risk issues named earlier could apply to the networked access control system in Figure 4-2 as follows:

- **Denial of services (DOS).** A DOS attack could keep an organization from updating its access control server.

- **Insertion of inaccurate data.** Inserting an inaccurate record could give an unauthorized person access to a physical facility. A terrorist group could hack into a computer available on the network, and then grant access to an unauthorized card so their group could enter a shipping facility.

- **Data theft.** Someone could steal a company's records and find out who to socially engineer to obtain a badge. For example, someone could find out the name of an employee with appropriate access to the building, meet the employee in a bar, and surreptitiously copy the employee's badge.

- **Data modification.** Someone could modify a record and grant himself access where he should not have it. A system vulnerability could make the access system available on the network. For example, an employee could gain access to an inappropriate area of a bank by exploiting a system vulnerability and modifying his record to grant additional, unauthorized access permission.

- **Data destruction.** Some could destroy the trail of his access to a particular area of the company. For example, after accessing a sensitive area where check stock is stored, an internal employee could destroy the audit trail that showed he was there.

The two examples—a video system and an access control system—illustrate that when physical security devices are placed onto the corporate network, the security professional must manage an increased set of risks. The next section discuss a variety of types of attacks against networked security systems.

4.2   COMMUNICATIONS ATTACKS

Once the security systems are communicating on the network, they are susceptible to attack. These attacks can come via multiple vectors. Here are some of the possibilities:

Social engineering: Someone convinces a user to share his credentials to get on the network.

Direct hacking: Someone goes after a system, by directly accessing it via normal channels or by exploiting a vulnerability.

Malware: Someone attacks a system by installing software on it, either with the user's knowledge (usually hidden in other software or e-mail) or automatically, without the user's knowledge.

Web attack: Some portion of the Web interface with the user (like browsing to a Web page) allows for accessing the system.

4.2.1 SOCIAL ENGINEERING

Social engineering is the manipulation of people to get them to do something that weakens the security of the network. One of the ways criminals use social engineering is to convince people to give up their user IDs and passwords.

In the case of a video recording system, certain users are able to access the system. Usually, they need to enter a username and password (in many cases, the same one they use to access the network). Many companies also make the software available from remote locations, over the Internet. Certainly, it is convenient for a number of people to be able to access the video at any time, no matter their location.

However, without appropriate controls, the video recording software could be compromised. In a common social engineering attack, a hacker calls up, pretends to be from the IT department, and tells the user to divulge his password so the system can be fixed. If the user is not appropriately educated (or is a helpful person by nature) he will give up his user name and password. The intruder can now easily access the recording system.

An access control system might run on a Web server on the Internet ("cloud computing"), or instead it might run on an internal server. Either way, a hacker could gain access to the access control server by using socially engineered credentials. Once in, he could create his own credentials or perhaps even open a door.

4.2.2 DIRECT HACKING

In a direct hacking attack, a hacker works with tools under his control to gain access to the network. The physical security analogy for this is the bank robber who tunnels into a vault to steal the money. He is directly involved in the crime. Similarly, the hacker needs to identify what defenses are in place and then defeat them. The fewer defenses that are in place, the more easily the hacker can compromise the system.

Regarding the video recording software, hackers are likely to start by checking a readily accessible Web site. If they can steal the password via social engineering, they will.

If not, they might use a brute force password cracker that enables them to try many passwords very quickly. However, many systems now have tools that lock out hackers after trying too many password.

Next, hackers look for vulnerabilities (program flaws that allow people to do things they should not). Typically, they use free, automated tools to exploit those vulnerabilities. In the case of a server running a video recording system, a hacker could leverage an unknown or unrepaired flaw in the system to gain access to the machine and create an account for himself or change a password.

In some cases, even a completely "patched," up-to-date system can become vulnerable. An engineer could configure the system incorrectly or make an architectural mistake, such as plugging an internal server into a switch that is accessible via the Internet.

The consequences are identical to those of social engineering. With full access to a system, a hacker can do whatever a system administrator can—that is, anything.

4.2.3 MALWARE

One of the most insidious mechanisms hackers use today to attack systems is malware. Malware—viruses, worms, spyware, rootkits, Trojan horses, etc.—is designed to give the cybercriminal or hacker control of the computer on which it is installed. Malware often circumvents preventive measures. These are among the reasons:

- Antivirus software is not kept up-to-date.

- Untrained users open booby-trapped e-mails and files or visit booby-trapped Internet sites.

- System administrators allow users to install software on the desktop.

Malware can install itself either as part of other software, automatically when e-mail is displayed, and by several other methods. It is particularly insidious because its designers program it to be primarily silent. In the earlier days of hacking, hackers wanted to make a statement—they wanted people to know they took over a machine. Now many hackers are interested solely in financial gain. The longer they can stay in stealth mode, owning an organization's systems and stealing its information, the more they can gain.

The first thing a hacker needs is access to the system. There are typically two mechanisms for gaining access with malware. A general attack focuses on obtaining access to any system and might give a hacker access to a system; a focused attack targets a specific individual and takes such steps as passing back information to an intruder or allowing for remote control of the system.

Workstations inside the network are usually protected by a firewall and VPN, so they may not appear to be immediately accessible. However, users can receive malware in a number of ways: from an e-mail, by loading a piece of software, or through a Web-based attack. Once malware has been loaded on a computer, it can grant remote control to a hacker or perform whatever it is programmed to do.

Once a criminal has taken control of a user's workstation, especially if he captures the user's passwords, he can do anything the user can do, including taking control of physical security system.

4.2.4 **WEB ATTACKS**

Web attacks can focus on clients (user workstations, for example) or on servers (gaining direct, unauthorized access to system resources and information). A Web attack is particularly dangerous because it can defeat almost every control.

Regarding client attacks, when users are accessing the Web they can pick up malware simply by going to a compromised Web site. A number of sites, some of them big brand names, have been compromised with malware in the past. For example, in 2010 malicious code was added to sites hosted by Network Solutions (Krebs, 2010).

Once a user goes to a Web site on which malware has been inserted, malware could be loaded onto the user's computer even if the user does not click on anything (because a Web browser executes code on a Web page automatically).

Hackers also attack Web sites to obtain information on the individuals who visit those sites. The Open Web Application Security Project (http://www.owasp.org) periodically publishes a top 10 list of Web attacks. The following are types of flaws commonly found on Web sites, allowing hackers unauthorized access or control:

Injection

Injection flaws, particularly Structured Query Language (SQL) injection, are common in Web applications. Injection allows an attacker to execute a command directly on a database contrary to allowed access rights. Users typically can only enter data, not commands. An SQL injection attack occurs when a hacker is able to send input to a server via a form field or URL that gives the server an instruction to return information that it should not return.

Cross-site scripting (XSS)

A cross-site scripting error on a Web site allows an attacker to run malicious code from a second Web site (controlled by the cybercriminal) on the browser of the person viewing the first Web site. This malicious code can do whatever the cybercriminal has programmed it to do, including installing a Trojan horse on the user's computer.

Broken authentication and session management

This class of vulnerabilities allows cybercriminals to compromise passwords, keys, or authentication tokens to assume a legitimate user's identity.

Insecure direct object references

A failure to prohibit direct access to the internal "objects"—files, directories, programs, etc.—on a Web server can lead to illegitimate use of the server.

Cross-site request forgery (CSRF)

Cross-site request forgery is an attack where the victim's browser is tricked into issuing a command to a vulnerable Web application. Unlike cross-site scripting (XSS), which exploits the trust a user has for a particular site, CSRF exploits the trust that a site has in a user's browser.

Security misconfiguration

When a Web server or application is not configured in accordance with appropriate security requirements, it is then subject to attack and compromise affecting confidentiality, integrity, and availability.

Insecure cryptographic storage

Cryptographic keys and other cryptography elements must be securely stored so they cannot be compromised. (It was an insecure cryptographic storage vulnerability that led to TJ MAXX's loss of 34 million credit card numbers.)

Failure to restrict URL access

While Web sites often have sub-pages that are not shown to users without access rights (admin pages, for example), if there's a failure to restrict URL access, a cybercriminal can type the suspected URL directly into the browser's URL bar, thereby gaining illegitimate access to the pages.

Insufficient transport layer protection

Web sites that do not protect data in transit with Secure Sockets Layer (SSL) or Transport Layer Security (TLS) are vulnerable to traffic interception and modification.

Unvalidated redirects and forwards

Web applications often redirect and forward users to other sites and pages. A redirect or forward should be validated by the server before it is executed. If the redirect or forward is not validated by the server, then a cybercriminal can compromise the intended redirect or forward, redirecting victims to phishing or malware sites or using forwards to access unauthorized pages.

Many organizations leverage Web application platforms, using a Web server interface that runs software that is accessed via a Web browser. In the Web interface, after users log in, they can interact with the application. For example, a user might call up an access record to make modifications. In poorly written code, such a query might be a part of the URL—for example, http://www.yourcompany.com/query.asp?employeeid=5551111.

If the software is not written securely, putting incorrect data in the query (for example, http://www.yourcompany.com/query.asp?employeeid=999999'99) might divulge whether it is possible to obtain more data. If the server and application are improperly configured, they may return a set of error messages. By examining the error messages, a hacker could create appropriate commands for the next query, which might look like this:

www.yourcompany.com/query.asp?employeeid=99999999'%20or%201=1--

Depending on the database and the application, this query could tell the database to return the incorrect employee's record or else records to which the hacker should not have access. A command sent to the database could divulge the database's contents, destroying it, or take control of the server.

Security professionals should examine whether their systems are susceptible to such attacks, find out how to fix the code (in-house or via a vendor), and whether any mitigating controls can be put in the middle.

4.3 **INFORMATION SECURITY MANAGEMENT SYSTEM**

Physical security professionals mitigate risk via policies, references, and frameworks. ISS professionals mitigate risk through an information security management system (ISMS), such as that described in ISO 27001 and 27002.

As authors writing in the *ISSA Journal* note (Lam, Pease, Stahl, & Takamine, 2007):

> In today's world, everyone is at risk from cyber crime. And, it will take us all to lower the risk to acceptable levels. Information systems security no longer simply involves those working in the field as professionals.

Physical security professionals can contribute both risk management and security perspectives to the protective effort.

According to ISO 27001, the following are essential elements of an ISMS:

- the existence of an information security management system (ISMS)
- the appropriateness of any system in place for the organization
- ongoing risk identification and management
- incorporation of appropriate controls into the ISMS
- appropriate monitoring, review, maintenance, and improvement of the ISMS
- appropriate management responsibility
- internal auditing or review
- management review of the ISMS

The first job of the individual charged with an organization's ISS is to create an ISMS appropriate for the size of the organization. If the ISO ISMS is not a good fit, one can find good ISS templates for small businesses on-line.

Next ongoing risk assessment, which makes it possible to identify any new risks and plan for controls or countermeasures. This is a common process in physical security; in ISS it is a more fluid process, as risks change significantly and continually. Appropriate controls must be put in place initially and then constantly updated to address the changing landscape. For example, a firewall might have been a sufficient control 20 years ago, but it is no longer so.

Appropriate management responsibility for the ISMS must be in place in each organization. This typically means assigning the role of chief information security officer (CISO) to an individual, preferably full-time. To strengthen the organization's ISS culture, senior management must support the process. Management should actually be concerned about

ISS. For example, the CEO could be given a quarterly report on ISS. In addition, senior management should assign internal audit roles to make sure the ISMS is doing what it needs to do. The CISO could report directly to the audit committee.

It is critical for the physical security professional to collaborate with the ISS department to ensure that physical security is a good ISS partner and complies with policies and procedures.

ISO 27002 (p. 4) lists the following elements as critical to the success of an ISMS:

- security policy
- organization of ISS
- asset management
- human resources security
- physical and environmental security
- communications and operations management
- access control
- information systems acquisition, development, and maintenance
- information security incident management
- business continuity management
- compliance

4.3.1 SECURITY POLICY

Without a policy, it is difficult to tell people what they should do to be secure. The creation of a security policy is typically a multidisciplinary, multidepartment function. Physical security participation is critical for two reasons. First, ISS policy affect day-to-day physical security operations (both staff's interaction with computers and security devices' connections to and interaction with the network). Second, ISS policy defines what types of devices are allowed on the network. Some physical security devices are not mature from an ISS perspective; participation in ISS policy creation and updating may help ensure that physical security concerns are addressed and appropriate physical security elements are selected.

4.3.2 ORGANIZATION OF ISS

Some elements of ISS organization are familiar to physical security professionals, such as contacts with law enforcement and special-interest groups. Some ISS-specific issues include system access and third-party review.

Regarding video surveillance, a security professional might want a vendor to configure the cameras. To talk to those cameras, the vendor may need access to the organization's network. To get such access, the vendor likely needs authentication, which means the vendor needs credentials. Authentication may also be needed for the actual physical security hardware. If the organization outsources video system management, ISMS policies must apply to the vendor, as well.

Similarly, as cloud computing becomes more prevalent (allowing third parties access to an organization's systems or information), cloud providers must adhere to the organization's policies, and physical security professionals should make sure those vendors are in compliance. In most cases, before a third party can have access to an organization's data, it must go through a vetting process. That process should ensure that its ISMS is appropriate for the data being shared and that the client will be able to audit the vendor in the future.

4.3.3 ASSET MANAGEMENT

This deals with the special requirements for information as it is transmitted on the network and stored on devices that reside on the network. Some physical security-related information may need special handling. Video could contain highly sensitive content that needs to be specially protected. An access control system contains the keys to an organization's doors and must have special controls in place to make sure it is not compromised.

4.3.4 HUMAN RESOURCES MANAGEMENT

The necessary background checks, terms of employment screening, security awareness and training, disciplinary process, and termination practices in an ISMS context are similar to what a physical security practitioner already knows. Because physical security practitioners have a mature understanding of human resources management, they can contribute much in this arena.

4.3.5 PHYSICAL AND ENVIRONMENTAL SECURITY

On this matter, clearly, the physical security practitioner can and should offer his expertise to help the ISS practitioner. The ability to secure areas in which ISS assets reside is critical to protecting those assets. Likewise, it would harm the organization if an access control or video recording server were stolen. As collaboration between physical and logical security increases, better solutions will result for all involved.

4.3.6 **COMMUNICATIONS AND OPERATIONS MANAGEMENT**

Communications and operations management deals with many issues that must be addressed from a security perspective (ISO 27002, pp. 37-59):

- computer system turn-on
- computer system shutdown
- emergency shutdown procedures
- change management
- segregation of duties
- third-party service delivery
- capacity management
- system management
- system acceptance
- malicious code protection
- system backup
- network security controls
- media handling
- security of system documentation
- exchange of information
- on-line transactions
- monitoring
- clock synchronization

Computer System Turn-On, Shutdown, and Emergency Shutdown Procedure

Computer-based systems may take unexpectedly long to start up and shut down. In older video surveillance systems, after a power loss was restored, video cameras would turn on right away and connect via coaxial cable to a recorder. In the event of a failure in a modern system, a number of systems may need to come up in a certain order, including servers, storage area networks, and Internet connections. Those systems may need to wait for power to be on for a certain amount of time (for a generator to charge the batteries on an uninterruptible power supply) or they may face certain failures that were not a consideration previously. The physical security practitioner benefits from understanding these limitations and planning for them.

Similarly, computer systems can take a lot longer to turn off. Cycling (restarting) a system in the event of a problem could pose significant issues, such as leaving an organization's video system down during the restart.

Other emergencies can force a system shutdown. A water leak, for example, may require an entire computer room to be shut down. Although in an analog setting one might have been able simply to move the digital video recorder (DVR) to another location, it is not be possible to carry away an entire server room, especially if multiple systems are involved in operating the video system. One solution is to have another server room available at a different location to take over the operations of recording those cameras.

Change Management

Change management is fundamental to IT, and it can seriously affect physical security operations. For example, physical security units cannot simply upgrade their access control systems without having a conversation with IT. A change can affect the entire network. Upgrading a video camera, for example, could cause a broadcast storm on the network due to a bug in the camera, causing not only that video camera but also other systems to stop working.

Conversely, IT departments must work with physical security professionals to ensure that changes made to the network do not adversely affect physical security assets. For example, an upgrade to a server operating system may prevent the access control server software from functioning properly.

Segregation of Duties

Segregation of duties is also familiar to many physical security practitioners. In the IT context, it is important to understand that some of the systems to which physical security practitioners have access are highly sensitive. In an access control system, users can create their own credentials to access virtually any area of the company. Without a separation of duties, the same person who has access to create access control cards might be the same person who is patrolling a building and should not be going inside with unauthorized access.

Third-Party Service Delivery

From an operational perspective, because third parties can now provide services, all service-level agreements in place for internal providers should also be in place for the third parties. Critical systems are critical regardless of who provides them. For example, an outsourced video provider should be required to have enough bandwidth to display the organization's video 24 hours a day. ISS professionals can help ensure that the organization is protected with service-level agreements.

Capacity Management

In a modern video environment, normal video may flow to a single workstation only. In an emergency, significant numbers of people may need to see the video, including across the

Internet. If these operational concerns are not expressed in advance, the necessary bandwidth will not be in place. From a security perspective, the A in CIA would be violated, as the system would not be available, rendering it useless at that time.

System Management

Systems that run on computers have specific needs that were not necessarily critical when they were embedded systems. For example, systems now need to be patched to fix problems with the software. This can mean that a particular system can be out of commission temporarily. The physical security practitioner needs to consider whether or not an asset (such as a critical camera)can be allowed to be down. If not, there may be a way to keep that camera functional, or it might be possible to install a temporary replacement. In some instances, it may be desirable to have multiple cameras focused on one location to ensure that the new paradigm does not get in the way of operational critical elements of a system.

System Acceptance

System acceptance is the process of making sure systems are up to specification. It is useful process for end-users (the people who actually use the product), but is also a requirement for ISS staff to ensure systems that go on the network are not going to compromise the network or other devices connected to it. Physical security practitioners should be prepared to go through the process of acceptance to make sure that they are getting what they want and that the system is safe for the network.

Malicious Code Protection

Viruses, Trojan horses, and other pieces of malicious code can render systems and entire networks inoperable. In the case of access control, not placing antivirus or other host protection software on the machine that runs the system could leave it susceptible to compromise or failure. Worse, that machine could bring down an entire network. Physical security systems need to have protections for such attacks, and those protections need to be updated.

System Backup

Computers are machines with moving parts, and they may occasionally fail. If data is not backed up, it could be lost. An organization might have a compliance requirement to retain video for a certain period, so it needs to back that data up in case of hardware or system failure. Regarding access control software, if it is not backed up and data is lost, it may have to be reconfigured by hand, rendering the system inoperative for a period, causing a denial of service and possibly leading to repair costs from a consultant.

Network Security Controls

Security systems need to comply with particular types of technologies and controls. For example, a DVR that is not properly designed might not have appropriate security for being on the network. Additionally, if cameras are not ".1x compliant," they might not be able to securely attach to the network.

Media Handling

Data can exist on various media, such as hard drives, USB sticks, or tape backups. Security professional should consider how critical the data is and what they can do to protect it, both from being lost and from being compromised. For example, it could be disastrous if someone stole a USB drive containing video important to an ongoing investigation.

Security of System Documentation

A critical need is the importance of protecting system documentation. If hackers obtain the documentation for an organization's access control software, they may be able to figure out how to create and add unauthorized proximity cards. If they know how an organization operates its video camera system, they may be able to view both recorded and live video to figure out how to compromise the facility.

Exchange of Information

It is often helpful to exchange information with first responders. However, they may not be fully aware of the implications of accessing an organization's data over the Internet. A company might want local police to have access to its video in the event of a terrorist attack, but it would not want them to share the log-in credentials inappropriately. People who are given access to an organization's systems must be trained in security policies so they do not compromise the system.

On-Line Transactions

If a company provides on-line services or electronic commerce transactions, it must apply the appropriate industry standards, policies, and procedures, as well as be compliant with any relevant laws and regulations. Many companies have been given sanctions for not having appropriate ISS management systems or policies while conducting e-commerce.

Monitoring

Just as physical security professionals monitor the perimeter of the buildings, ISS professionals monitor various aspects of the network and their systems, looking at logs (making sure the firewall is not being attacked) and looking at machines (making sure they are not compromised).

Clock Synchronization

A notable practice in ISS is clock synchronization. This is typically done with a protocol called Network Time Protocol (NTP), and it allows for all systems on a network to have the same time. When correlating events on the network, whether a physical security intrusion, a network attack, or even setting the time on a video surveillance system, for evidence purposes it is important that all the elements record the same time.

4.3.7 ACCESS CONTROL

Security systems that reside on a network, such as video surveillance and physical access control systems, require logical access control of some sort. A user name/password mechanism may not be sufficient given the sensitivity and criticality of the information stored on the system. Physical security professionals should discuss this issue with ISS specialists so that security data will be treated as critical.

Access control is also a familiar concept to the physical security practitioner. The idea is to let in only those people who are authorized, after appropriate identification. In physical security, this is typically done with a security officer, a key, or an access card.

Because someone can now access a company's systems from across the world, identity verification is vital. For example, a physical security provider may want to make video available on the Internet. However, corporate ISS policies prohibit accessing confidential information without using second-factor authentication. Second-factor authentication uses something like a one-time password or a fingerprint scanner to make it much more difficult for someone to enter a system.

This situation makes vendor selection more complex, because the preferred service provider may not offer second-factor authentication. The vendor may be good from a physical security perspective and bad from an ISS perspective. The physical security professional should work with ISS experts to reach an appropriate decision.

Another issue is that the access control server that the security department wants to place on the network may run an operating system that does not adhere to corporate security policy. It may be unable to appropriately authenticate users, leaving the system susceptible to attack, or it may be an old, outdated operating system with unpatchable vulnerabilities.

4.3.8 **INFORMATION SYSTEMS ACQUISITION, DEVELOPMENT, AND MAINTENANCE**

As a security operation acquires new systems, develops new software, or upgrades existing systems, it must make sure none of those actions expose the organization to undue risk or create a problem in any part of the CIA triad: confidentiality, integrity, or availability.

Regarding video cameras, for example, the security professional should make sure the video recording shows what is really happening and the camera views are available all the time. Furthermore, it is important to encrypt the video stream and ensure that whenever credentials are passed between a workstation and the device, they cannot be easily stolen off the network. Otherwise, the organization may face one of these familiar issues: denial of services, insertion of inaccurate data, data theft, data modification, and data destruction.

4.3.9 **INFORMATION SECURITY INCIDENT MANAGEMENT**

With regard to information security incident management, physical security practitioners can be of assistance as they have large-scale practice with dealing with incidents. Forensic examiners, who are often critical to the incident response process, also often come from the physical security realm.

Physical security practitioners may be particularly interested in the legal aspects of information security incident management, specifically regarding evidence from a seized computer, server, or network trace.

4.3.10 **BUSINESS CONTINUITY MANAGEMENT**

As business continuity is planned, there are numerous areas of involvement for the physical security practitioner.

First, physical security technology assets required for operation need to be able to continue to run in the event of an unexpected incident. For example, IT must continue to provide video surveillance services to physical security departments so they can maintain security. If analytics are unavailable because they were not properly planned for in a state of emergency, then the security of a company can be compromised when these tools are needed the most. In the event that power is not available, it is important that network-based systems, such as access control, maintain functionality.

Second, personnel still need to be available in the event of an emergency. Physical security personnel are often well-versed in taking care of these types of logistical needs, such as how to house a large number of people for an extended period. So, the active participation of the physical security professional can be a critical help to ISS practitioners.

Third, an off-site venue may be needed as part of the business continuity plan. If so, physical security staff can work with ISS and IT staff to make sure the venue is secure, available, and able to accommodate staff.

4.3.11 COMPLIANCE

Some compliance issues directly affect both physical security and ISS. First, some decisions on security may be nonnegotiable from a legal perspective. For example, certain government organizations must have a specific level of access controls in place. Organizations under the jurisdiction of Sarbanes-Oxley (SOX) must meet other requirements to be in compliance.

It is critical for the physical security professional to fully understand this aspect of the security policy so as not to place other systems at risk or take the chance that his own systems fail in a way that causes the company to be out of compliance.

4.3.12 ISMS SUMMARY

This review of the elements of an ISMS examined numerous junctions where the physical security practitioner and the ISS practitioner can benefit from working together. Many examples have been provided to show how ISS is critical to securing physical security assets in a converged environment. At the same time, vulnerable physical security elements can weaken ISS. By understanding the ISMS and working within its framework alongside ISS, physical security professionals can gain the benefits of convergence while mitigating risk.

4.4 **CONCLUSION**

As organizations continue the process of convergence to realize the benefits of incorporating security systems into the network infrastructure, the security of physical assets become intertwined with the security of information systems. Insecurities in converging physical and information systems enlarge the risk portfolio against which the physical security professional must respond. They need a protected data stream, whether the stream is a point-to-point cable or goes across the network.

Convergence in security highlights the importance of joining the physical security paradigm, the point-of-view of the physical security practitioner, to that of the information systems security practitioner's counterpart, the logical security paradigm. To address the new challenge, physical security professionals must (Lam & Stahl, 2010)

augment their Physical Security Paradigm with a new Logical Security Paradigm appropriate for dealing with the unique, never-before-seen challenges of information systems security.

Physical security professionals should talk with their ISS colleagues, understand ISS problems and the logical security paradigm that infuses that work, and share the physical security paradigm with ISS staff. Top management, too, can play a role in integrating the physical and logical security paradigms in an organization.

REFERENCES

ISO 27001. (2005). *Information technology—security techniques—information security management systems—requirements.* Geneva, Switzerland: International Organisation for Standardization.

ISO 27002. (2005). *Information technology—security techniques—code of practice for information security management.* Geneva, Switzerland: International Organisation for Standardization.

Krebs, B. (2010). Network Solutions again under siege. Krebs on Security. Available: http://krebsonsecurity.com/2010/04/network-solutions-again-under-siege [2010, December 5].

Lam, D., Pease, K., Stahl, S., & Takamine, K. (2007, July). Creating the information security village. *ISSA Journal.*

Lam, D., & Stahl, S. (2010, January). Convergence, paradigm shifts and reaching the village. *ISSA Journal.*

Tyson, D. (2007). *Security convergence: Managing enterprise security risk.* Burlington, MA: Butterworth-Heinemann.

INDEX

A

AAA Triad, 103–104, 120
Access control, 13, 23–26, 34, 38, 74–77, 91, 120, 162–169, 173, 181. *See also* Networked access control
Acquisition, 182
Administrative controls, 90
ANSIR. *See* Awareness of National Security Issues and Response Program
Anti-forensics, 67
Antivirus software, 26, 66, 171–172
Applicability, 32
Application development security, 120
Application layer, of OSI model, 100
Application security, 27
Approval process, 17
ASIS. *See* Information Asset Protection Council
Asset management, 176
ATM machines, 78
Audits, 12, 20, 24, 34, 176
Authentication, 13, 63, 91, 103–104, 172, 176, 181
Automated systems, 13
Awareness, 11–12, 147–148
Awareness of National Security Issues and Response (ANSIR) Program, 3

B

Backup, 6, 105, 179–180
Banks, 63–64, 135, 136–138
Barriers, 15
BCP. *See* Business continuity plan
Blogs, 151
Boards of directors, 121–122
Botnets, 78
Buffer overflow, 101
Business continuity plan (BCP), 16, 120, 182–183
Business impacts, 9–10
Business intelligence collection, 2–3
Business practices, 16
Business process, 1

C

Cable locks, 18
California Senate Bill 1386, 64
Calling cards, 112
Capacity management, 178–179
Card reader, 163
CBP. *See* Customs and Border Protection, U.S.
CD-ROM, 96
Cell phones, 28, 114. *See also specific types*
CERT. *See* Community Emergency Response Team
Certificates, 116
Certified Information Systems Security Professional (CISSP), 120, 150
Change management, 178
Chief information security officer (CISO), 174–175
Children's Online Privacy Protection Act (COPPA), 127–128
China, 2, 22
CIA Triad, 104, 182
CISO. *See* Chief information security officer
CISSP. *See* Certified Information Systems Security Professional
Class action suits, 138
Classification, 32–33, 38–42, 70
Clock synchronization, 181
Cloud computing, 108, 169, 176
Cold War, 3, 5
Common Body of Knowledge, 120–121
Common Vulnerabilities and Exposures (CVE), 117
Communications, computer, 98–99, 164–166
Communications attacks, 169–173
Communications management, 177
Community Emergency Response Team (CERT), 149
Community-based countermeasures, 92
Competitive advantage, 9–10, 39
Compliance, 90, 183
Computability, 93
Computer logic entry points, 100–101
Computer operation, 95
Computer scripts, 88

Computer security, 26–27, 65, 66, 70

Computer systems, 7, 64, 79, 94–105, 107–114, 177–178

Conception, 51–54

Confidentiality, 12, 25, 45–48, 85, 90, 104–105, 182

Continuity plan. *See* Business continuity plan

Contracts, 24, 25, 29

Controller, 163

Convergence, 159–184

Cookies, 135

Copiers, 110

COPPA. *See* Children's Online Privacy Protection Act

Copyrights, 20, 21, 22, 37

Cost of crime, 63, 78

Counterespionage, 4

Counterfeiting, 8–9, 20

Counterintelligence Domain Program, 3

Countermeasure, 26, 86, 90–92, 174

Covered Accounts, 130

CRC. *See* Cyclical redundancy check

Credit cards, 123–124, 132–133, 135

Crime, 71. *See also* Cyber crime

Cross-site request forgery (CSRF), 172

Cross-site scripting (XSS), 62, 171

Cryptography, 120

CSRF. *See* Cross-site request forgery

Culture, 16, 147–148, 174

Customs and Border Protection, U.S. (CBP), 20

CVE. *See* Common Vulnerabilities and Exposures

Cyber crime, 61, 65–68, 78–79, 88, 92, 98, 109, 136–138, 144

Cyber extortion, 65

Cyber terrorism, 88

Cyclical redundancy check (CRC), 105

D

Data, insertion of inaccurate, 159–161, 167

Data backup, 6, 105, 179–180

Data destruction, 42, 55–56, 159–161, 168

Data input challenges, 100–101

Data link level, of OSI model, 97–98

Data loss protection (DLP), 117

Data mining, 6–7

Data modification, 159–160, 161, 168

Data Protection Directive, 21, 135–136

Data theft, 159–160, 161, 167

DECA. *See* Developing Espionage and Counterintelligence Awareness Program

Decryption, 93, 116

Defense-in-depth. *See* Layered protection

Denial of services (DOS), 159–160, 161, 167

Department of Commerce, U.S., 135–136, 149

Department of Health and Human Services, U.S. (HHS), 125, 133

Destruction, 42, 55–56, 159–161, 168

Detection, 90

Developing Espionage and Counterintelligence Awareness (DECA) Program, 3

Device protection security, 91

Digital signature, 27

Direct communication, of computers, 98–99, 164–166

Disaster recovery plan (DRP), 120

Disposal, 42, 55–56

DLP. *See* Data loss protection

Document markings, 42

DOS. *See* Denial of services

DRP. *See* Disaster recovery plan

Due diligence, 9, 15, 16, 25, 29, 55–56

Dumpster diving, 5, 55

E

E-conferencing, 28

Economic Espionage Act (EEA), 3

Economic security, 78

Economics, of ISS, 68–69

EEA. *See* Economic Espionage Act

802.1x, 117

Electronic documents, 42

Electronic files, 18

Electronic transfer, 42

E-mail, 42, 108–109, 171

E-mail gateway, 116

Embedded controller, 163

Embedded systems, 73

Emergency shutdown procedure, 177–178

An Emerging Information Security Standard of Due Care (Braun & Stahl), 69
Employee privacy, 34
Employee training, 16, 92
Encryption, 27, 105, 134
Equation, Fundamental ISS, 87
Espionage, 2–5, 7–8
EU. *See* European Union
European Union (EU), 16, 21, 135–136
Exchange, of information, 180
Executive management, 69, 89, 92, 121–122
Extended Enterprise, 38
External information, 12
Extortion, 65
Extrusion prevention, 27

F

FACT. *See* Fair and Accurate Credit Transaction Act
Fair and Accurate Credit Transaction (FACT) Act, 129
Fax machines, 18, 42, 114
Federal Trade Commission, U.S. (FTC), 16, 128–134
File transfer protocol (FTP), 109
Fingerprint scanner, 181
Firewall, 26–27, 66, 68, 107, 117, 171
Firmware, 36, 95
Foreign governments, 16, 29
FTC. *See* Federal Trade Commission, U.S.
FTC Act, 131–132
FTP. *See* File transfer protocol

G

GAISP. *See* Generally Accepted Information Security Practices
General Accountability Office, U.S., 8–9
Generally Accepted Information Security Practices (GAISP), 122
GIAC. *See* Global Information Assurance Certification
GLBA. *See* Gramm-Leach-Blilely Act

Global Information Assurance Certification (GIAC), 150
Global information environment, 4–5
Globalization, 4–5
Gramm-Leach-Blilely Act (GLBA), 126–127, 130–131
Guideline on Information Asset Protection, 11, 39

H

Hackers, 62–63, 65, 66, 67, 71, 96, 98, 108, 109, 169–171
Hardware, 36, 95
Health Information Technology for Economic and Clinical Health (HITECH) Act, 125
Health Insurance Portability and Accountability Act (HIPAA), 21, 125, 133, 139
Heartland Payment Systems, 124, 138
HHS. *See* Department of Health and Human Services, U.S.
Highly restricted information, 32, 38–42
HIPAA. *See* Health Insurance Portability and Accountability Act
HIPS. *See* Host intrusion protection systems
HITECH. *See* Health Information Technology for Economic and Clinical Health Act
Host intrusion protection systems (HIPS), 116
Host-based systems, 73
Hosts, 101–104

I

IAP. *See* Information asset protection
IAP program manager, 31–32, 33
Identification, 12, 66, 74
Identity theft, 28, 129–130, 138
Identity Theft Prevention Program (Program), 129–130
IDF. *See* Intermediate Distribution Facility
IDS. *See* Intrusion Detection System
Inadvertent threats, 6
Incident database, 30
Incident management, 182
Incident response, 142–143

Industrial espionage. *See* Espionage

Information, highly restricted, 32, 38–42

Information asset protection (IAP), 1, 4–10, 38–41

Information Asset Protection Council (ASIS), 1, 3, 11, 39, 149

Information asset protection policy. *See* Policy

Information assets, 1, 2, 32

Information classification, 32–33, 38–42, 70

Information loss, 29–30, 37, 50, 117

Information revolution, 7

Information risk management, 4–10, 17, 68, 120

Information security governance, 120–122

Information security management system (ISMS), 118–119, 139, 144–146, 174–181

Information security policies, 11–12, 31–38, 69, 141, 175

Information security technologies, 116–117

Information sharing, 16, 32–33, 35, 38, 42

Information storage. *See* Storage

Information Systems Audit and Control Association (ISAC), 149

Information systems control objectives, 90

Information systems countermeasures, 26, 86, 90–92, 174

Information systems infrastructure, 89, 91, 106

Information systems management processes, 89

Information systems security metrics, 92

Information systems threat, 5–8, 11, 86, 87–89

Information Technology (IT), 26–27

InfraGard, 149

Infrastructure, 89, 91, 106

Infringement, 21, 23, 25

Injection, 172

Inputs, 100–101

Insecure cryptographic storage, 172

Insecure direct object references, 172

Insertion of inaccurate data, 159–161, 167

Insiders, 7–8

Integrity, 85, 90, 105, 182

Intellectual property, 21, 22, 24–25, 29, 61

Intellectual Property Rights e-Recordation program, 20

Intentional threats, 5–6

Intermediate Distribution Facility (IDF), 97

Intermediate project phases, 49–50

Internal information, 12, 38–42

International concerns, 24–25

International Organization for Standardization, 96, 118–119

Internet, 7, 20, 37, 64, 71, 77, 78, 107, 113, 161, 169, 177. *See also* Center for Internet Security

Internet Protocol (IP), 96

Internet Storm Center, 86

Intranet, 42

Intrusion Detection System (IDS), 27, 116

Intrusion Prevention Systems (IPS), 116

IP. *See* Internet Protocol

IPS. *See* Intrusion Prevention Systems

"Is Your Model Non-Disclosure Agreement Adequate?", 43

ISAC. *See* Information Systems Audit and Control Association

ISMS. *See* Information security management system

ISO/IEC, 118–119, 139

ISSA Journal, 92

IT. *See* Information Technology

IT Infrastructure Library (ITIL), 106

IT resources, 36

IT security, 26–27

ITIL. *See* IT Infrastructure Library

J

Judicial decisions, 68

K

Keyloggers, 89

Koobface, 89

L

Laboratory notebooks, 49–54

LAN. *See* Local area network

Laptops, 28, 36, 102

Law enforcement, 17, 20, 130–134, 176

Laws, 3, 20, 22, 23, 29, 37, 42, 64, 70, 90, 123–138
Lawsuits, 137–138
Layered protection, 12–13, 26
Legal issues, of ISS, 123–138, 151
Local area network (LAN), 27
Logical network access control, 27
Log-in field, 101
Loss, 29–30, 37, 50, 117

M

Mail, 42
Maintenance, 182
Malicious code protection, 178
Malware, 63, 66, 67, 71, 78, 116, 137, 170–171, 179
Management, 144–148. *See also specific types*
Management countermeasures, 92
Managing technical reports, 49–50
Marketing, 22, 89, 148
Marketing spyware, 89
Marking, protected information, 12, 42
Media handling, 180
Meeting security, 18–20
Metrics, ISS, 92
Microcomputer revolution, 64, 79
Microsoft Windows, 95
Microsoft Word, 109
Misconfiguration, 172
Misprints, 13
Mobile devices, 28, 36, 67, 102, 114
Mobile malware, 67
Monitoring, 180–181
Multi-factor authentication, 63
"Mutual Non-Disclosure Agreement," 45

N

NAC. *See* Network access control
National Counterintelligence Executive, 5, 18
National Institute of Standards and Technology (NIST), 149
National security, 79
National Security Decision Directive, 17

National Vulnerability Database, 117
Natural disasters, 6, 87
Natural threats, 6
NDAs. *See* Nondisclosure agreements
Network access control (NAC), 117
Network layer, of OSI model, 99
Network risk, 159–168
Network security, 26, 70, 78, 180
Network Time Protocol (NTP), 181
Networked access control system, 76–77, 162–168
Networked video system, 160–161
NIST. *See* National Institute of Standards and Technology
Nondisclosure agreements (NDAs), 20, 24, 25, 29, 32–33, 37, 38, 43–48
NTP. *See* Network Time Protocol
Nuclear weapons, 3

O

One time password (OTP), 104
On-Line transactions, 180
Open Systems Interconnect (OSI), 96–100
Open Web Application Security Project (OWASP), 149
Operating systems, 95
Operations security (OPSEC), 17, 120
Organizational loyalty, 8
OSAC. *See* Overseas Security Advisory Board
OSI. *See* Open Systems Interconnect
OTP. *See* One time password
Overseas Security Advisory Council (OSAC), 2, 5, 18
OWASP. *See* Open Web Application Security Project

P

Passwords, 26, 62, 101, 104, 108, 109, 148, 169, 181
Patch management, 27
Patents, 2–3, 21, 23, 37
Payment Card Industry Data Security Standard (PCI DSS), 13, 115, 123–124, 139

PBX. *See* Private branch exchange
PCI DSS. *See* Payment Card Industry Data Security Standard
PDAs. *See* Personal digital assistants
PDCA. *See* Plan-do-check-act model
Perimeter security, 91
Peripheral information, 17
Personal digital assistants (PDAs), 28, 102, 114
Personal identification numbers (PINs), 66
Personnel security, 15, 70
Phishing, 65, 71, 78
Physical barriers, 15
Physical controls, 90
Physical layer, of OSI model, 97
Physical security, 12–15, 24, 61, 70, 71–77, 92, 105, 109–110, 114, 121, 143, 175, 176–177, 181, 182
Physical security information manager (PSIM), 116
PINs. *See* Personal identification numbers
Piracy, 8–9
Plain old telephone service (POTS), 111
PlainsCapital bank, 137
Plan-do-check-act (PDCA) model, 145–146
Policy, 11–12, 31–38, 69, 141, 175
POTS. *See* Plain old telephone service
Practitioner framework, 118–122
PRC. *See* Privacy Rights Clearinghouse
Presentation layer, of OSI model, 100
Printers, 110
Privacy, 15–16, 34, 64, 98, 126–128, 134–135, 138
Privacy Act, 21
Privacy Rights Clearinghouse (PRC), 64, 150
Private branch exchange (PBX), 110–111, 113
Processors, 96
Production, 14–15
Program. *See* Identity Theft Prevention Program
Program manager, 31–32, 33
Programming, 101
Proprietary information, 44–45
Protected information, markings of, 12
Protection requirements, 42
Prototypes, 14
Proximity card, 74
Proxy servers, 117

PSIM. *See* Physical security information manager
Public information, 17
Public release of information, 35

Q

QoS. *See* Quality of service
Quality of service (QoS), 115
Quick reference guide, 39–42

R

Records, 13–14, 55–56
Recovery, 29–30, 90
Recycling, 55
Red Flags Rule, 129–130
Red Queen Effect, 144
Redirects, unvalidated, 17
Reduction, to practice, 51–54
Reed Elsevier (REI), 132–133
Registration, 21, 23
Regulations, of ISS, 123–138
Regulatory Compliance Planning Guide, 21
REI. *See* Reed Elsevier
Remote maintenance and administration terminal (RMAT), 111
Reputation, 1, 9
Residual threat risk, 87
Restricted information, 32, 38–42
Reverse engineering, 3
Risk assessment process, 4, 9, 70, 139–140, 174
Risk management, 4–10, 17, 68, 120
Risk mitigation, 11–20
Risk monitoring, 9
Risks, ISS, 86–92, 159–168
RMAT. *See* Remote maintenance and administration terminal
Rogueware, 67
Root cause analysis, 30
Rootkits, 171
Router, 99, 166

S

Safeguarding Proprietary Information Council, 3
Sanitizing, 27
SANS. *See* System Administration, Networking, and Security Institute
Sarbanes-Oxley Law (SOX), 128–129, 183
SCADA. *See* Supervisory control and data acquisition
Scanning, 110
SEC. *See* Securities and Exchange Commission
Section 404, of SOX, 128
Securities and Exchange Commission (SEC), 128
Security, 12–15, 17, 18–20, 24, 61, 70, 71–77. *See also specific types*
Security, of system documentation, 19, 24, 180
Security architecture, 121
Security awareness/training, 35, 94-96, 144, 151-153, 161, 180
Security convergence, 159–184
Security governance, 120–122
Security misconfiguration, 172
Security reviews, 29
Segregation, of duties, 178
Seisint, 132–133
Seminars, 18
Servers, 102
Service-level agreement (SLA), 106
Session layer, of OSI model, 100
Session management, 172
Settlements, of FTC, 132–134
Seven Layer Network Model (OSI), 96–100
Shredders, 13
Shutdown, 177–178
SLA. *See* Service-level agreement
Smartphones. *See* Cell phones
Social engineering, 169
Social networking, 89
Social Security numbers, 28, 62, 68
Software, 26, 28, 36, 173
SOX. *See* Sarbanes-Oxley Law
Spam, 116
Special environments, 28
Special topics, of ISS, 139–144
Spoofing, 78
Spy networks, 5

Spyware, 71, 78, 89, 171
SQL. *See* Structured Query Language injection
Stand-alone computing device, 96
Standards, 12, 34, 87, 90, 110, 115, 117-118, 122-123, 126, 129, 134-135, 139, 141, 149
State breach disclosure, 134–135
Storage, 7, 14, 42, 56, 172
Structured Query Language (SQL) injection, 171
Supervisory control and data acquisition (SCADA), 71
Surveillance, 26, 72–73, 160–161, 176, 181, 182
Switches, 98
System acceptance, 179
System Administration, Networking, and Security Institute (SANS), 86, 150
System backup, 6, 105, 179–180
System management, 178
System monitoring, 91

T

Targeting, 18
TCP/IP. *See* Transmission control protocol/Internet protocol
Technical controls, 90
Technical protective measures, 26–29
Technical reports, 49–54
Technical surveillance countermeasures (TSCM), 26
Technology, 10, 13, 78, 94. *See also* Information Technology
Telecommunications, 26, 110–114, 121
Temporary files, 18
Terrorism, 7, 62, 65, 71, 79, 88
Third-party information security assurance, 70
Third-party review, 115
Third-party service delivery, 178
Threats, 5–8, 11, 86, 87–89
Timeline, of technology-based commercial product, 50
Trade secrets, 23, 24, 37, 50
Trademarks, 20, 21, 23, 37
Transmission control protocol/Internet protocol (TCP/IP), 73, 76, 77, 96
Transport layer, of OSI model, 100
Travel security, 7, 18–20, 35–36

Trends in Proprietary Information Loss, 6, 7
Triads, 103–104, 120, 182
Trojan horse, 63, 89, 116, 171, 179
TSCM. *See* Technical surveillance
        countermeasures
Turing Machine, 79, 93
Twitter, 65

U

UL. *See* Underwriters Laboratories
Underwriters Laboratories (UL), 73
Uniform Commercial Code, 137
United States Computer Emergency Readiness
        Team (US-CERT), 66
United States v. Carroll Towing Co., 68
Unrestricted information, 33, 38–41
URL access, 173
US-CERT. *See* United States Computer
        Emergency Readiness Team
User awareness, 69
Usernames, 26, 62, 101, 108, 109, 169
Users, 89, 105

V

Version control, 38
Vetting procedures, 15
Video infrastructure, 72
Video recording system, 169, 170
Video surveillance, 26, 72–73, 160–161, 176,
        181, 182
Video-to-Recorder layout, 72
Virtual private network (VPN), 107, 108, 161, 171
Virtual threats, 88–89
Viruses, 64, 68, 71, 116, 171, 179
Visual barriers, 15
Voicemail, 110
Voice-over-IP (VOIP), 111–113
VPN. *See* Virtual private network
Vulnerabilities, 4, 17, 86, 88–93, 108–109, 117,
        139–140, 170, 181
Vulnerability and patch management, 91

W

WAF. *See* Web application firewall
Warning notifications, 24
Web application, 108, 149
Web application firewall (WAF), 117
Web attacks, 171–173
Web gateway, 117
Web pages, 117
Web presence, 37
Web sites, 62–63, 127–128, 171–172
Weigand protocol, 73, 75
Wireless hot spots, 28
Wireless local area networks (WLAN), 27
Wireless networks, 65
Wireless Watch, 43
WLAN. *See* Wireless local area networks
Workstations, 102
World Trade Center, 62
Worms, 71, 89, 116, 171

X

XSS. *See* Cross-site scripting

Y

YouTube, 65

Z

Zeus (trojan horse), 89